MW01657239

CANDYFREAK

Also by Steve Almond

My Life in Heavy Metal

CANDYFREAK

A Journey through the Chocolate Underbelly of America

STEVE ALMOND

ALGONQUIN BOOKS OF CHAPEL HILL 2004

Published by
ALGONQUIN BOOKS OF CHAPEL HILL
Post Office Box 2225
Chapel Hill, North Carolina 27515-2225

a division of
Workman Publishing
708 Broadway
New York, New York 10003

Printed in the United States of America.
Published simultaneously in Canada by
Thomas Allen & Son Limited.
Design by Rebecca Giménez.

Portions of this book have appeared in slightly
different form in the *Boston Phoenix*.

Library of Congress Cataloging-in-Publication Data
Almond, Steve.
Candyfreak : a journey through the chocolate underbelly of America /
by Steve Almond.—1st ed.
p. cm.
ISBN 1-56512-421-9
1. Candy industry—United States. 2. Candy. 3. Chocolate.
4. Almond, Steve. I. Title.
HD9330.C653U513 2004
338.4'7664153'0973—dc22 2003070801

10 9 8 7 6 5 4 3 2
First Edition

TO DON RICCI ALMOND,

a freak of unparalleled wisdom and

sweetness. I love you, Pop.

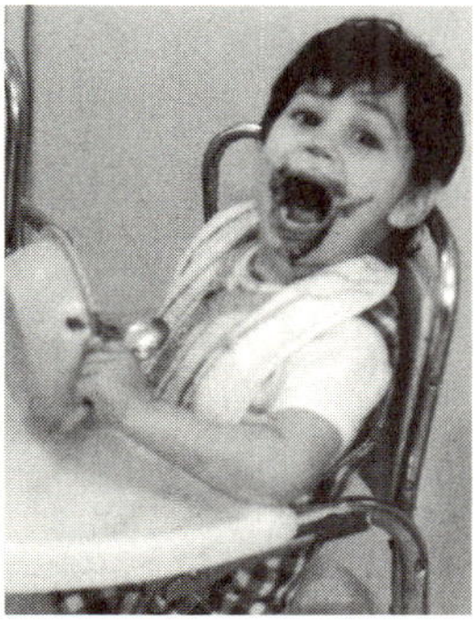

PHOTO BY DON RICCI ALMOND, 1968

See, only a chocolate Jesus

Will satisfy my soul.

TOM WAITS

CONTENTS

CHAPTER SIX

CHAPTER SEVEN

CHAPTER EIGHT

CHAPTER NINE

CHAPTER TEN

CHAPTER ELEVEN

CHAPTER TWELVE

CANDYFREAK

PROLOGUE

SOME THINGS YOU SHOULD KNOW ABOUT THE AUTHOR

1. The author has eaten a piece of candy every single day of his entire life.

I want you to look at this sentence and think about it briefly and, if you're so inclined, perhaps say a little prayer on behalf of my molars. This would not be unwarranted, and for supporting evidence I refer you to Elizabeth Gulevich, a highly competent doctor of dental surgery who spent most of the early seventies numbing my jaw. I doubt Dr. Gulevich is the sort to have established a hall of fame in her waiting room (she was more the Ansel Adams type) but I would like to believe that my run of seven cavities during the infamous campaign of 1973 stands as some kind of record.

Not a single day did I *fail to consume,* not one, not during those miserable family camping trips to Desolation Wilderness during which I kept nervous vigil over the trail mix for its meager ration of M&M's; nor at Camp Tawonga, where I learned to savor the sweet gnash of hickeys and sun-ripened Red Vines; nor on those days when I was cut off from outside supply lines, bereft of funds, during which I thieved chocolate chips from the baking shelf and pressed same into a spoonful of Jif peanut butter; nor even in the aftermath of the removal of all four of my impacted wisdom teeth by a gentleman whose name was, I believe, Dr. Robago (Italian: *butcher*), after which I was on liquid food for five days and therefore partook of shakes from the Peninsula Creamery, made with mint chip ice cream.

Also, was I the only child in America who regarded Baker's Chocolate as the cruelest food product ever invented? Was I the only one who—despite repeated warnings from the Mother Unit, despite the dark knowledge that the Mother Unit would not knowingly place a pound of chocolate within my reach, that this was simply *too easy,* despite even my own clear memory of having tried this stunt before and wound up with a mouthful of bitter goo—reached into the back of the cupboard and removed the box and greedily slipped a square from its curiously stiff, white wrapper? Was I the only one who gazed upon the thick, angled square, so much like a Chunky, really, in abject lust? And who held the piece to my nose and breathed in the deep brown scent and then, despite all the evidence to the contrary, simply unable to will my disbelief, bit down?

2. *The author thinks about candy at least once an hour.*

More than that, actually, and not just the eating of a particular piece of candy, but a consideration of potential candies. For several years, I've been obsessed with the idea of introducing a new candy bar into the market: a crisp wafer held together with hazelnut paste, topped by crushed hazelnuts, and enrobed in dark chocolate. My friends have listened to me rather patiently and only a few have been impertinent enough to point out that no one in America actually likes hazelnuts, a kibbitz to which I generally respond, *Yes, and they didn't like penicillin at first either, did they?*

I think, occasionally, about the worst candy bar I ever ate, purchased on an overnight bus trip from Istanbul to Izmir back in 1986 and which had a picture of a donkey on the wrapper (this should have been a red flag) and a thick strip of cardboard to make it seem bulkier and which tasted like rancid carob and had a consistency similar to the sandy stuff Dr. Gulevich used to blast between my teeth.

More often, though, I think about the candy bars of my youth that no longer exist, the Skrunch Bar, the Starbar, Summit, Milk Shake, Powerhouse, and more recent bars which have been wrongly pulled from the shelves—Hershey's sublime

Cookies 'n Mint leaps to mind—and I say kaddish for all of them.

And when I say I think about these bars I am not referring to some momentary pulsing of the nostalgia buds. I am talking about detailed considerations of how they looked and tasted, the whipped splendor of the Choco-Lite, whose tiny air pockets provided such a piquant crunch (the oral analogue to stomping on bubble wrap), the unprecedented marriage of peanuts and wafers in the Bar None, the surprising bulk of the Reggie!, little more than a giant peanut turtle, but round—a bar that dared to be round! Or, at the other extreme, the Marathon Bar, which stormed the racks in 1974, enjoyed a meteoric rise, died young, and left a beautiful corpse. The Marathon: a rope of caramel covered in chocolate, not even a solid piece that is, half air holes, an obvious rip-off to anyone who has mastered the basic Piagetian stages, but we couldn't resist the gimmick. And then, as if we weren't bamboozled enough, there was the sleek red package, which included a ruler on the back and thereby affirmed the First Rule of Male Adolescence: *If you give a teenage boy a candy bar with a ruler on the back of the package, he will measure his dick.*

Oh where are you now, you brave stupid bars of yore? Where Oompahs, those delectable doomed pods of chocolate and peanut butter? Where the molar-ripping Bit-O-Choc? And where Caravelle, a bar so dear to my heart that I remain, two decades after its extinction, in an active state of mourning?

Without necessarily intending to, I keep abreast of candy. I can tell you, for instance, that Hershey's introduced in the fall of 2002 a Kit Kat bar with dark chocolate. I spent two weeks searching for this bar, because I had tasted a similar bar fifteen years earlier when I lived in Jerusalem and, back then, the taste had made me dance in happy little nondenominational circles, flapping my arms. Why two weeks? Because giant candy companies like Hershey's rarely devote an entire production line to a new product without market testing, which means producing a *limited edition,* which means people like me (that is, candyfreaks) have to stop in every single Mobil station in the greater Boston area and ask the staff if they have Kit Kat Darks, because that is where my friend Alec told me he found his.

Well.

In the end, Alec—with whom I play squash, though, as a tandem, we somewhat belittle the definition of the sport—brought me a bar, purchased from the Inman Pharmacy, and I'm happy to report that it is absolutely mind-blowing. The dark chocolate coating lends the fine angles of the bar a dignified sheen and exudes a puddinglike creaminess, with coffee overtones. This more intense flavor provides a counterpoint to the slightly cloying wafer and filling. By the time you read this, Kit Kat Darks will very likely have been discontinued, because they failed to make a gazillion dollars, which is a sad thing for you, I promise, though not so much for me because, in an abundance of caution, I purchased fourteen boxes (36 bars per) soon after my first taste.

I can also tell you that Nestlé has introduced a Wonka Bar, which features crumbled bits of graham cracker in milk chocolate, and which to date I have only been able to find in my local movie theater. Last spring, Nestlé introduced a bar called the Mocha Crunch, which I spotted in a vending machine at Boston College, of all places, and I nearly wept with joy right there in the basement of the building where I teach college students how to write sentences far more coherent than this one, because I allowed myself to dream that the woefully neglected coffee flavor might finally be wending its way into the candy bar mainstream. I envisioned rich milk chocolate infused with the smoky tang of French roast. But the bar wasn't even made of chocolate. It was some kind of white chocolate compound that looked, and tasted, like vinyl.

3. *The author has between three and seven pounds of candy in his house at all times.*

Perhaps you think I am exaggerating for effect.

I am not exaggerating for effect.

Here is a catalog of all the candy in my apartment as of right now, 3:21 P.M., July 6, 2003:

- 2 pounds miniature Clark Bars
- 1.5 pounds dark chocolate–covered mint patties
- 24 bite-size peanut butter cups
- 1 pound Tootsie Roll Midgets
- 4 ounces of Altoids-like cinnamon disks
- 6 ounces cherry-flavored jellies (think budget Jujyfruits)
- A single gold-foiled milk chocolate ball with mysterious butter truffle–type filling
- 2 squares of Valrona semisweet chocolate (on my bedside table)
- 3 pieces Fleer bubblegum

I am not counting the fourteen boxes of Kit Kat Limited Edition Dark, which I have stored in an undisclosed warehouse location, nor whatever candy I might have stashed, squirrel-like, in obscure drawers.

My main supplier is the Candy Shoppe, a seconds outlet located on the ground floor of the Haviland Chocolate factory in Cambridge. The Shoppe is run by an elderly Chinese woman whom I've been wooing ardently for the past two years. We've gotten to the point where she's willing to cut open the box of mint patties I bring to the counter to make sure the batch I'm buying has the soft kind of filling I favor. She gives me freebies and glances at me occasionally in a squinting manner that combines reluctant affection with a deep, abiding pity.

I am not blind to the hypocrisy of my conduct, nor to the slightly pathetic aspects of my freakdom. I am, after all, in my mid-thirties, suffering from severe balding anxiety and lower-back pain. I am not exactly the target demographic. What's more, my political orientation is somewhere to the left of Christ, such that I find most of American culture greedy and heedless, most especially our blithe and relentless pigging of the world's resources. I have a hard time defending the production of candy, given that it is basically crack for children and makes them dependent in unwholesome ways, and given that much of our citizenry is bordering on obesity (just about what we deserve), and given that most of the folks who grow our sugar and cocoa are part of an indentured Third World workforce who earn enough, per annum, to buy maybe a Snickers bar and given that the giants of the candy industry are, even as I write this, doing everything in their considerable power to establish freak hegemony over what they call "developing markets," meaning hooking the children of Moscow and Beijing and Nairobi on their dastardly confections.

So, the question: Given all this moral knowledge, how can I lead the life of an unbridled candyfreak?

1

THE AUTHOR WILL NOW RATIONALIZE

The answer is that we don't choose our freaks, they choose us.

I don't mean this as some kind of hippy dippy aphorism about the power of fate. We may not understand why we freak on a particular food or band or sports team. We may have no conscious control over our allegiances. But they arise from our most sacred fears and desires and, as such, they represent the truest expression of our selves.

In my case, I should start with my father, as all sons must, particularly those, like me, who grew up in a state of semi-thwarted worship.

Richard Almond: eldest son to the sensationally famous political scientist, Gabriel Almond, husband to the lovely and formidable Mother Unit (Barbara), father to three sons, esteemed psychiatrist, author, singer, handsome, brilliant, yes, check, check, check, expert maker of candles and jam, weekend gardener, by all measures (other than his own) a stark, raving success. This was my dad on paper. In real life, he was much harder to figure out, because he didn't express his feelings very much, because he had come from a family in which emotional candor was frowned upon. So I took my clues where I could find them. And the most striking one I found was that he had an uncharacteristic weakness for sweets, that he was, in his own still-waters-run-deep kind of way, a candyfreak.

I loved that I would find my dad, on certain Saturday afternoons, during the single hour each week that his presence wasn't required elsewhere, making fudge in the scary black cast-iron skillet kept under the stove. I loved how he used a toothpick to test the consistency of the fudge and then gave the toothpick to me. I loved the fudge itself—dense, sugary, with a magical capacity to dissolve on the tongue.

Following his lead, I even made a couple of efforts to cook up my own candy. I would cite the Cherry Lollipop Debacle of 1976 as the most memorable, in that I came quite close to creating actual lollipops, if you somewhat broaden your conception of lollipops to include little red globs of corn syrup that stick to the freezer compartment in such a manner as to cause the Mother Unit to weep.

I loved that my dad was himself obsessed with marzipan (though I did not love marzipan). I loved his halvah habit (though I did not love halvah). I loved that he bought chocolate-covered graham crackers when he went shopping, and I do not mean the tragic Keebler variety, which are coated in a waxy, synthetic-chocolate coating that exudes a soapy aftertaste. I mean the original, old-school brand, covered in dark chocolate and filled not with an actual graham cracker, but with a lighter, crispier biscuit distinguished by its wheaty musk. I loved that my father would, after certain meals—say, those meals in which none of his sons threatened to kill another—give me a couple of bucks and send me to the Old Barrel to buy everyone a candy bar. What a sense of economic responsibility! Of filial devotion! I loved that my father chose Junior Mints and I loved how he ate them, slipping the box into his shirt pocket and fishing them out, one by one, with the crook of his index finger. I loved watching him eat these, patiently, with moist clicks of the tongue. I loved his mouth, the full, pillowy lips, the rakishly crooked teeth—the mouth of a closet sensualist.

It is worth noting the one story about my father's childhood that I remember most vividly, which is that his father used to send him out on Sunday mornings with six cents to get the *New York Times,* and that, on certain days, if he were feeling sufficient bravado, he would lose a penny down the sewer and buy a nickel pack of Necco wafers instead. This tale astounded me. Not only did it reveal my father as capable of subterfuge, but it suggested candy as his instrument of empowerment. (In later years, as shall be revealed, I myself became a prodigious shoplifter, though I tend to doubt that the legal authorities would deem the above facts exculpatory.)

The bottom line here is that candy was, for my father and then for me, one of the few permissible forms of self-love in a household that specialized in self-loathing. It would not be overstating the case to suggest that we both used candy as a kind of antidepressant.

There were other factors in play:

Oral Fixation—It is certainly possible that there is a person out there more orally fixated than me. I would not, however, want to meet him or her. We begin with thumbsucking. Oh yes. Devout thumbsucker, years zero to ten. I don't remember how I was weaned from this habit, though it was probably around the time my older brother, Dave, asked me if I wanted to feel something "really cool," then told me to put my hands behind my back and rubbed my thumbs with what felt like an oily towelette, but was, in fact, a hot chili plucked from the *ristra* hanging in our kitchen, which I discovered immediately upon sticking my thumb in my mouth. I was rendered speechless for the next four hours.

So I kicked the thumb, but took up lollipops, gum, Lick-A-Stix, hard candies, and Fruit Rolls, which I used to wrap around my fingers and suck until my knuckles turned pruney.

I still bite my nails to the quick. I've chewed through a forest of toothpicks. I've even tried to take up smoking. I frequently feel the desire to bite attractive women, not just in moments of *amour,* but in elevators, restaurants, subways.

I don't think of this as particularly strange. Babies, after all, learn to interact with the world through their mouths. For a good year or so—before their parents start hollering at them not to put things in their mouths—all they do is put things in their mouths. Perhaps my folks failed to yell this at me enough, because I still take on the world mouth-first, and I think about the experience of the world in my mouth all the time. (I am certain, by the way, that there is some really cool German word for this idea of the world in my mouth, something along the lines of *zietschaungundermoutton,* and if this were the sort of book that required actual research, I would consult my father, who speaks German.) What I mean by this is that I imagine what it would be like to lick or chew or suck a great deal of stuff. Examples would include the skin of a killer whale, any kind of bright acrylic paint, and Cameron Diaz's eyeballs.

I practice a good deal of mouthplay.

If for instance, I happened to be eating a Jolly Rancher Cherry Stick, which I happened to be doing for much of my youth, I would gradually shape the candy into a quasi retainer. This was done by warming the piece until malleable, then pressing it up into my palate with my tongue. At a certain point, this habit morphed into an ardent belief that I could use candy to straighten my teeth, which were (and are) crooked. This was not such a crazy idea. Braces, after all, operated on the basic principle that, if pushed hard enough, *teeth would move*. So I spent most of fifth and sixth grades with a variety of hard candies lodged between my upper teeth. Charm's Blow Pops were most effective for this purpose, because they had a stick and could thus be removed voluntarily.

The Whole Name Thing—You will have noticed by this time, that I have a distinctly candyfreakish name. This is not my fault. All credit or blame should be directed to my paternal great-grandfather, the Rabbi David Pruzhinski (blessed be his memory), who came from the region of Pruzhini to London around 1885 and changed his name to Almond. Why Almond? The official explanation is steeped in academic ambition. David took secular classes during the day then raced off to attend rabbinical classes at night. The professors at his college posted grades and assignments in alphabetical order. So he needed a new name that began with a letter at the beginning of the alphabet. No one knows why he settled on Almond over, say, Adams. There has been speculation that he was the victim of a prank. Or that he chose Almond because the almond tree is frequently mentioned in the Old Testament. Whatever the reason, I was saddled with this strange name, which meant that I was constantly, *constantly,* being serenaded with the *sometimes you feel like a nut* Almond Joy/Mounds jingle, which I would have liked to quote in full, except that Hershey's legal staff denied me permission. I can certainly understand why. God only knows what ruin might befall Hershey's if this jingle—which hasn't been used in two decades—were suddenly brazenly resurrected by a young Jewish candyfreak. One shudders to consider the fallout for the entire fragile candy-jingle-trademark ecosystem. The company was, however, thoughtful enough to include in its letter of refusal a coupon for a dollar off any Hershey's product—Twizzlers included!—which certainly went a long way toward restoring *my* faith in corporate America.

I should note that the success of this particular jingle was an undying source of fascination to me and especially irksome because I didn't even like almonds as a kid and absolutely loathed coconut, an enmity which will be discussed further on. I'm not suggesting that my identity was determined by something as random as my last name, just as I wouldn't suggest that those with the last name Miller will grow up with a predilection for cheap beer. But there is no doubt that having a name associated with candy was a contributing factor. So was the date of my birth, October 27, a mere four days before the Freak National Holiday. And one other fact that I have come to regard as eerie: for virtually my entire childhood our family lived on a street called Wilkie Way.

Freak Physiology—I have been endowed with one of those disgusting metabolisms that allow me to eat at will. To physiologists, I am a classic ectomorph, though my ex-girlfriends have tended to gravitate toward the term *scrawny*. The downside of this metabolic arrangement is that I am a slave to my blood sugar. If I don't eat for too long, I start thinking about murdering people, and I am inexorably drawn toward fats and carbs. I hate most vegetables, particularly what I call the evil brain trio—broccoli, cauliflower, brussels sprouts—which tastes, to me, like flatulence that has been allowed to blossom. Left to my own devices, my diet would consist of dark chocolate and baguettes, with perhaps a grilled pork rib thrown in for variety. I realize that I am going to hell.

Every now and again, I'll run into someone who claims not to like chocolate or other sweets, and while we live in a country where everyone has the right to eat what they want, I want to say for the record that I don't trust these people, that I think something is wrong with them, and that they're probably—this must be said—total duds in bed.

CHOCOLATE = ENABLER

The main thing, though, is that I formed this emotional bond to candy. My parents were too busy, my older brother wanted me dead, my twin brother set off into the world without me. This was how I saw things. I was a needy kid, and terribly lonely, and candy kept me company. I wasn't fat, but I understood the appeals of gluttony, how a certain frantic gratification might numb the sting of sorrow. And if it seems, at times, that I am playing off my obsession with candy as something frivolous/heartwarming, this is, like most of our routines, just a way of obscuring its darker associations.

I can remember staggering down the streets of Baden-Baden, Germany, at dawn, close to hysterical with an unnamed sadness. This was the summer between my sophomore and junior years in college. I was traveling in Europe because I assumed this was what one did at age 20 in order to acquire that mysterious attribute known as worldliness. Earlier in the day, I'd met some fellow travelers at a hostel and we'd smoked some hash and there was some girl involved, a blond Australian who I hoped might be willing to kiss me a little. But I did something uncool, let my desperation show, and they ditched me outside a fancy casino. I wandered back to the hostel, but it was closed for the night and when I tried to sneak in, a German fellow came and shouted at me in a manner that made me think of Hitler. So I spent the night walking from one end of town to the other. When I think about this episode, what returns to me most vividly is the elegant vending machine outside that casino, which sold Lindt chocolate bars for a single deutsche mark. And how, in the morning, I found an outdoor café and bought a roll which I cut in half and buttered to make a chocolate sandwich.

Years later, I moved to Poland to live with a woman. But we soon fell out of love and began to argue. In the evenings, after our fights, flushed and seething and scared to death, I would wander the narrow avenues of her town and stop at one of the kiosks to buy a candy bar, the name of which I don't remember, only that it was a sweet vanilla wafer covered in a dark, bitter chocolate. On the day I returned home to America, I found a cache of these bars at the bottom of my suitcase, left there by my lover, that I might carry with me, at least a little longer, the taste of our doomed enterprise.

IN WHICH AN UNHEALTHY PATTERN OF DEPENDENCE IS ESTABLISHED

We need to talk a little about the Initial Candy Supplier (ICS). Everyone has an ICS and in most cases people can recall not just the name but the smell of the place, the precise configuration of the racks, the quality of light across those racks. In the psychic galaxy of the child, the ICS is the sun.

My ICS was the aforementioned Old Barrel, a neighborhood landmark built around a tremendous, and presumably old, wine barrel, at least 20 feet tall. It was not until much later (age 30, actually) that the connection between this architectural flourish and the store's identity dawned on me. This is because I never thought of the Old Barrel as a liquor store. It was a candy store. I was fascinated by the barrel, though. For many years, I believed it was actually full of wine and I spent hours speculating as to what would happen if someone chopped through the weather-faded wood. Would the surrounding land be flooded with cheap cabernet? Would people drown? And furthermore, how did one remove wine from such a barrel? Was there some hidden spigot? As I have mentioned, I was a lonely child.

I knew all the guys who worked at the Old Barrel, though not by name. There was Bald Guy and Tremor Guy and Bad Breath Guy. Mustache Guy was the most intriguing. He had this beautiful lacquered seventies pompadour and mutton-chops and a blond mustache I would describe as pornoriffic. I remember him most distinctly, I think, because he was the one who was least attentive and therefore, the easiest to shoplift off. And I can remember, at seven or eight, my father cornering me and demanding to know where I got the Grape Stick I was innocently shaping into a retainer. He marched me all the way back to the Old Barrel (I was bawling) and made me fess up to Mustache Guy and remunerate him a dime.

The lone exception to the no-name rule was Jimmy Zucanti, who was maybe five years ahead of me in school and who once gave me a minor concussion during a game of tackle the pill and who, at a certain point, showed up behind the counter. This was a stupefying development: the equivalent of having an acquaintance anointed pope.

The Old Barrel sold all the basics, your major candy bars, your LifeSavers and gums, your ten-cent quick-and-dirties (Hot Tamales, Jawbreakers, Lemonheads, Red Hots, Mike and Ike). But at a certain point, I needed to broaden my horizons.

Patterson's Drugs, on El Camino, stocked a candy known as Kits, tiny individually wrapped taffies that came four to a pack. Kits were smaller than Now and Laters and sweeter, and to my way of thinking, more distinguished. The packages were these perfect little rectangles, pink for strawberry, yellow for banana, brown for chocolate. I picked up 20 packs for a dollar and spent the balance of the afternoon playing with them on my bed.

This is generally what I did with candy: I played with it on my bed. I counted it. I organized it by color. I ran my fingers through it. I sat there like a pint-sized Midas and gloried in my wealth. Occasionally, I staged a kind of candy combat. I wasn't mindless about candy. I was ritualized.

At about age ten, during a late summer visit to Sears to buy school clothes, I became aware of the concept of candy by the pound. This was revolutionary. Here were entire *stalls* of candy, naked as the day they were born, piled up two feet high and God knows how deep, glittering behind glass windows. You might have thought I was staring at tropical fish in an aquarium. Or you might have been the poor clerk forced to sit inside the Sears candy stand on one of the many ensuing Saturdays, which meant you faced an odd decision: whether or not to call security on the little, bubble-eyed goon circling your station, which was me.

What it was—beauty. The sheer, entropic plenitude of gumdrops, jelly beans, orange slices. I might buy any of these, merely for the joy of watching the clerk dig her shiny little silver scoop into the bin, pouring out my portion first in a great plinking rush, then one by one *(plunk, plunk)* as the green numbers on the electronic scale blinked up. Mostly it was saltwater taffy, which was relatively light and therefore cheap and came in nine color-coded flavors, all of which, somewhat pathetically, I recall in precise detail: the pink-and-red swirled cinnamons, green-ribboned spearmints, the chocolate drops with blurry dabs of cherry in the center.

At Sears, candy prices were governed by the law of supply

and demand, especially after the seasonal candy rush. So, for example, the Christmas Mix reached a low point of 25 cents per pound if you waited until the second week of January. *(Dr. Gulevich: Are you sure he hasn't been eating candy? The Mother Unit: I don't see how. He only gets 50 cents allowance, and we don't let the boys eat sweet cereal.)*

At a certain point, of course, kids are supposed to outgrow candy. They move on to other freaks. My older brother, for instance, graduated from LEGOs to Estes rockets to beekeeping. Not me. By the early teenage years, I was making sojourns to the distant Mayfield Mall for a particular piece found only in the Kandy Karousel on level three. This was the mint parfait, two square slabs of bittersweet chocolate around a pale green center. Think a jumbo-size Andes mint, though with a sharper bite to the chocolate and none of that chalky aftertaste that plagues the Andes oeuvre. The parfait was a highbrow piece, and it amazes me a little to realize that I would ride my bike four miles each way and spend up to three dollars for a small white sack of them.

The discovery of marijuana more or less sealed my freak. I was never a burnout in the classic sense, meaning that I never grew my hair long and listened to Blue Öyster Cult and cut classes to hang out by the big oak tree next to the amphitheater. I was too terrified of academic failure to offer that sort of commitment. I tended to steal pot from my older brother and to smoke it alone, because smoking was something he did, something vaguely illicit, and though the quality of the weed was so poor that it would probably cause Snoop Dogg to go into anaphylactic shock, it did allow me to feel a gauzy sense of appreciation for the blessings in my life, chief amongst them candy. If I had been the kind of kid who kept a diary, the entries from the years twelve to say, sixteen, would have read: *Got high, ate candy.*

I remember, in this phase, eating a lot of Tangy Taffy. Wherefore Tangy Taffy? Because it was cheap. You could buy two slabs for 50 cents. They were tart enough to excite the salivary glands, a crucial factor in the battle against cottonmouth. Also, when buying a batch of candy—and by this time I was buying in batches—I liked to create a value gradient, such that I could eat the cheap stuff first and save the higher quality chocolate items for last. As for the actual taste of Tangy Taffy . . . imagine, if you will, a fruit-flavored caulk. Add some citric acid. Add some coloring. You're getting close.

As should be evident, candy was my chief extracurricular activity. This is not to suggest that I didn't do my share of candy worship in school. For a while there, before the Mother Unit got wise, I was given a buck fifty for lunch every day. The assumption was that I would buy, oh, I don't know, cauliflower sprigs or something. What I bought was Granny Goose Nacho Cheese Chips, chocolate milk, and the fascinating new

Twix bar, which I consumed by scraping the chocolate-and-caramel top layer off with my teeth, then sucking the remaining wafer-and-chocolate slab until it became a sugary mush.

Despite this diet, I eventually hit puberty and even underwent a do-at-home bar mitzvah (at age fourteen), which was not held in an actual hot tub, though I have from time to time told people this. For those of you not familiar with the mystical ways of the suburban Jew, the bar mitzvah is the ceremony whereby a boy delivers an achingly dull speech, mangles a few prayers in Hebrew, and thereby becomes a man. And just how did I commemorate this sacred passage into adulthood?

Got high, ate candy.

AN ILL-ADVISED DISCUSSION OF FREAK ECONOMICS

In the ideal world, moms and dads would have enough time and energy to fill their children with love, and brothers would take care of one another, and there would be lots of extended family members around to pick up the slack. But as it is, the developed world has become a cold, atomized place in which people are cut off from their internal lives and therefore subject to the most basic form of self-esteem extortion—materialism—which means that they have agreed to be judged by what they eat and wear and drive, by their fitness as capitalists, as opposed to, say, the content of their characters.

And this goes for children as well, who are, if anything, more apt to project their emotional life onto objects rather than people. Any parent whose child has a favorite blankie or sippy cup will back me up on this. What the folks in the boardrooms and on Madison Avenue sussed out a couple of decades back is this: *manipulation of family dynamics = big bucks.* Thus, the guilty dad will buy off his kid. And the deprived child will learn to seek love in material form.

Just as important, the folks whose job it is to move product (which is virtually all of us) have come to recognize that children are ideal consumers: impatient and dogged and ferociously brand loyal. Kids are also exquisitely attuned to the chaotic emotional rhythms of supply and demand. For what, in the end, was the mania surrounding baseball cards or Cabbage Patch Kids, if not a stock market in miniature? Or, better yet, Pokemon cards? If you ever spoke to a child in the thrall of Pokemon, you were basically talking to a day trader in vitro. Because these cards, in fact, had no utilitarian value. Their value was, as the wonks would put it, market determined. That market, while initiated by adults, was sustained entirely by kids.

Candy is the Dow Jones of the kid economy. And anyone who grew up during the sweaty seventies (as I did) can tell you about the various boom and bust cycles. I would cite the Bubble Yum craze of 1975 as paramount. Prior to this, your bubble gum genre had been ruled by either Bazooka (a solid-tasting, if somewhat grainy nostalgia product sold as piece candy) or Rain-Blo (loudly colored gum balls that came in clear plastic wrappers). Bubble Yum marked an innovation of both form and content. The manufacturers intuited that one of the limiting factors for the bubble gum market was that the product seemed too immature. So they created a package that resembled a candy bar, with five individually wrapped cubes. The gum itself was smooth, almost creamy, and loaded with sugar.

The response was astonishing. For months, all anyone could talk about was Bubble Yum. The most popular girls in my junior high school carried packs in the back pockets of their jeans, which were so tight as to allow a view of the contours. (Thus to be seen packing.) Guys gave girls two-packs as the official seal of going-steadydom. The rich kids from Los Altos Hills would celebrate birthdays with entire boxes. Bubble Yum was de rigueur at dances, where close physical proximity to the opposite sex was an actual possibility. Oh, to be a teenage lover smuggling his boner onto the dance floor during "When the Lights Go Down in the City" without a piece to honey the breath!

The Old Barrel couldn't even keep Bubble Yum stocked because the manufacturer couldn't keep the Old Barrel stocked. One had to journey further out into the retail market. And this led, of course, to the black market effect. Guys like Bobby

Hankey—who, it was rumored, had blown up a kitten—stockpiled Bubble Yum, then resold the stuff at considerable markup near the lockers. *(Bubble Yum dealers, dear, and right here in Palo Alto!)*

The mania reached such a pitch that an urban myth arose: Someone had found spider eggs in his Bubble Yum. I'm certain this was nonsense, just as I am relatively certain that Rod Stewart's stomach was not really pumped as a result of the ingestion of . . . oh, do I really have to go there? But the rumor struck me as meaningful nonetheless—an expression of communal guilt over our own rabid greed, and perhaps also a way of connecting to the larger world, to the other towns beset by the same contagion. Not even the emergence of various pretenders, such as Hubba Bubba and Bubblicious, could diminish our passion.

As dramatic as the Bubble Yum boom was, the Pop Rocks freak-out, a few years later, was ten times worse. Pop Rocks, for those who have never heard of them, are tiny fruit-flavored candies that come in the shape of finely ground gravel. They're like any other hard candy—a boiled blend of sugar, corn syrup, flavor, and coloring—except for the secret ingredient: carbon dioxide gas compressed at 600 pounds per square inch. As the candy cools, the pressurized gas is released and shatters the candy. But there are still tiny bubbles of pressurized carbon dioxide inside each of the shards. (You can see them with a magnifying glass.) And when these shards melt in someone's mouth, the gas bubbles pop. And I mean *pop*. Not just some soggy Rice Krispies–type pop, but a sound like fat crackling on a skillet—explosions, actual explosions, which registered seismically in the teeth, particularly if, like me, one decided to chomp down onto the Pop Rocks and not just let them dissolve on the tongue. Not only that, but Pop Rocks tasted good, sweet and fruity, and the different colors (cherry, grape, orange) actually had distinct flavors, not that it mattered especially because, my God, they exploded! A candy that explodes! No one had ever heard of such a thing. We were all instantly nuts.

Pop Rocks came in little packets, like vegetable seeds, and they cost up to a dollar a pack. Rather than discouraging us, this exorbitance merely enhanced their standing. They assumed a kind of mythic place in the pantheon of our economy—like saffron or high-grade uranium. Again, the result was furious black market activity. The Bobby Hankeys of the world bought up cases and sold them from the trunks of cars. My friend Evan, who lived in Connecticut, where Pop Rocks had not yet entered the market, had his aunt send him a box from California, which he resold at a nifty profit. An urban myth quickly grew up around the frenzy. To wit: that the snot-nosed child TV star Mason Reese had ingested lethal amounts of Pop Rocks and Coke, causing his stomach to explode. (In certain quarters, this rumor named Mikey of Life Cereal fame as the victim.)

By high school, the furor had shifted to gummy bears and later Jelly Bellys, both of which I consumed in embarrassing quantities, as a result, in part, of having taken a job at Edy's Ice Cream, where both were sold in bulk. Gummy bears, in particular, suggested a certain sangfroid, because they were German. I tended to burn them with matches, thus combining my overt sugarlust with a more latent strain of pyromania. I loved the way the little gummy bear heads would sizzle and smoke, and the syrupy consistency of the resulting mess. I spent a considerable portion of my ninth-grade science class (best estimate: 40 percent) scorching the heads off gummy bears with the fabulous, empowering Bunsen burner.

My point here is that the candy economy has always been driven by the peculiar, streaky passions of children. Over the past five years, the market for extreme candies has skyrocketed. Back in my day, extreme was represented by a candy called Zotz, which were mildly flavored hard candies filled with a citrusy powder that fizzed on the tongue. The modern Warhead, by contrast, is so sour it's impossible to keep in your mouth, unless you happen to be a nine-year-old boy determined to keep a Warhead in your mouth longer than your friend.

At last year's Candy Expo, there was quite a buzz surrounding the Torcher Scorcher, which is a kind of Atomic Fireball gone apocalyptic. It is no longer rare to see candies with cayenne pepper and chilies. To me, this is taking things way too far in the direction of candy machismo/masochism. Then again, the Mother Unit said the same thing when I came home with a candy that exploded in my mouth.

NIGHT OF THE LIVING FREAK

The rhythms of freak are ruled by the holiday calendar, and specifically by Halloween, which as we all know, can be traced back to All Hallows' Eve, an ancient religious rite in which priests raced around the streets of Dublin throwing snack-size Snickers bars at impoverished children.

This is what I love about Halloween. It has, from a freak perspective, purity of intent. There's no dallying about with God, or that contrived brand of devotion used to justify our other seasonal pageants of gluttony. There's something incredibly liberating about a holiday that *encourages* children to take candy from strangers.

Today, of course, our paranoia about child safety has reached this fabulous zenith whereby kids are only allowed to trick-or-treat accompanied by an adult and each piece of received candy is promptly and assiduously inspected with a metal detector and/or chemical toxicity kit. I watch the kids tromping about my neighborhood with their hawkeyed chaperones and I feel sorry for the poor little dudes. They hit maybe five houses an hour because the parents make each stop a little event, with thank-yous and much time spent admiring costumes and discussing the truly atrocious crimes that might befall children at any moment in these woeful days of ruination.

But back in the blithe, porno-soaked, latch-key seventies, the idea of trick-or-treating with a parent in tow was unthinkable—like publicly disclosing a preference for Barry Manilow. And yes, we heard plenty of tales about creepy old men sinking razors into caramel apples. But this only added an allure of risk to the endeavor. (As Bobby Hankey used to put it: *Don't bite down if the blade is facing outward, dickweed.*) We enjoyed the prospect of visiting iffy-looking houses and apartment complexes, because the people there had no sense of proportion and they led lives of mystery, amid their mysterious smells, and we could peek inside their homes at the strange artwork and the absence of furniture, and occasionally some guy would open the door in his underwear and throw quarters at us. This is how we learned about the world.

For the true freak, Halloween was all about game-planning. You couldn't just wander around, because you had a three-hour window and every minute counted and more important than that you had this remarkable concept known as Freak Amnesty, which meant, on this one evening, that you were allowed to gather and consume as much candy as you could without parental objection.

Come 6:30, I knew exactly where I was headed: up Wilkie Way toward Charleston, north onto Alma and back around to Meadow, with detours onto the densely packed streets surrounding Ventura, then to the skeezy apartments on James. I stayed away from fancy costumes, as these provoked discussion, and discussion was not what you wanted. You wanted a quick exchange. One year, I wrapped a bed sheet around me and went as . . . what? A Roman. A mummy. Origami. It was never quite clear.

I raced from house to house, sore-shouldered and gasping, past the idiotic pumpkin smashers and egg chuckers, to the lit doorsteps, where a basket of candy would be presented for my princely consideration. So I proceeded until ten, with special emphasis on that final hour, when the crowds thin out and the benefactors, having invariably overstocked and now fretting the surplus, grow exorbitant.

Now: I'm a great lover of visual art and I will happily discuss the color and texture of Van Gogh's *Starry Night*, or the way in which the eye is led into Goya's *The Third of May 1808*, and even though I don't really know what I'm talking about, I can get myself awfully worked up, just as a fine sentence or paragraph (say, the opening salvo of *Henderson the Rain King*) can send me into shivery rapture. But I can think of nothing on earth so beautiful as the final haul on Halloween night, which, for me, was ten to fifteen pounds of candy, a riot of colored wrappers and hopeful fonts, snub-nosed chocolate bars and SweeTARTS, the seductive rattle of Jujyfruits and Good & Plenty and lollipop sticks all akimbo, the foil ends of mini LifeSavers packs twinkling like dimes, and a thick sugary perfume rising up from the pillowcase.

And more so, the pleasure of pouring out the contents onto the rug in the TV room, of cataloging the take according to a strict Freak Hierarchy, calling for all chocolate products to be immediately quarantined, sorted, and closely guarded, with higher-quality fruit chews and caramels next, then hard candies, and last of all anything organic (the loathsome raisins). A brief period of barter with my brothers might ensue. For the most part, I simply lay amid my trove and occasionally massed the candy into a pile which I could sort of dive into, à la Scrooge McDuck and his gold ducats.

Again: I realize I was sick.

For me, the crisis arose at about age fourteen, when it occurred to me that I was at least a foot taller than the other trick-or-treaters and that my elaborately polite pleas for candy were now being viewed as a kind of extortion.

MISTAKES WERE MADE

I hope I haven't made my desires sound indiscriminate. They are not. When I disapprove of a candy, the sentiment often veers into wrath. A part of me wants to take the manufacturers by the short hairs and bitchslap some sense into them, though the real issue, obviously, is demand. It's the consumers who are responsible, in the end, for the abominations of the Freak Kingdom.

The one candy whose success is most puzzling to me is Twizzlers. Twizzlers is basically an imitation of red licorice, which, itself, has no cognate in the natural world. The defenders of this candy will probably object at this point, arguing that the most popular Twizzlers flavor is actually strawberry. In fact, Twizzlers bears roughly the same chemical relationship to strawberry as the Vienna Sausage does to filet mignon. Which is to say: none. Its flavor is so completely artificial that I've often wondered if the production staff might not endeavor to make it just a little more artificial, thus crossing over an invisible flavor threshold and allowing the product to start tasting *less* artificial. This is to say nothing of the Twizzlers texture, which falls somewhere between chitin and rain poncho.

As a former Tangy Taffy user, I realize that I'm not exactly on solid ground as an arbiter of taste. But I can at least plead youthful indiscretion on that count, whereas I continue to encounter grown men and women (some of them otherwise desirable) who blithely chomp at their Twizzlers cud, breathing their plasticine reek onto the rest of us.

To me, Twizzlers belongs to the same loathsome genus as the Jujubes. The young and fortunate reader may not have heard of Jujubes, and this candy will be hard to describe in a fashion that makes it sound suitable for human consumption. They were basically hard pellets the size and shape of pencil erasers. Indeed, if one were to set Jujubes beside pencil erasers in a blind taste test, it would be tough to make a distinction, except that pencil erasers have more natural fruit flavor.

These are two examples of candies I refer to as MWMs (Mistakes Were Made). Other would include:

Marshmallow Peeps: A candy that encourages the notion that it is acceptable to eat child offspring. Composed of marshmallow dyed piss yellow and sprinkled with sugar.

Circus Peanuts: Again, a marshmallow pretending to be something else, this time a legume. An affront to elephants everywhere.

Boston Baked Beans: If you are an actual peanut, why are you not covered in chocolate? Why are you covered, instead, in some kind of burnt-tasting brick red shell? Is the idea that you resemble a baked bean supposed to make you more alluring?

Jordan Almonds: Who chose the color scheme, Zsa Zsa Gabor?

Chuckles: A fruit jelly the consistency of cartilage. Explain.

Sixlets: Those of us over the age of, say, three can usually differentiate between chocolate and brown wax.

White jelly beans: I defy you to tell me what flavor white is supposed to signify. Pineapple? Coconut? Isopropyl?

Lime LifeSavers: The LifeSavers people haven't figured out by now that no one likes this flavor?

Coconut: We now come to an area where I depart from the rational and enter the realm of the phobic. Oddly, it isn't the flavor of coconut that troubles me, but the texture, and specifically that stringy residue utterly impervious to the normal processes of digestion. In short, I feel as if I'm chewing on a sweetened cuticle. Anyone who's eaten a Mounds knows exactly what I'm talking about. The chocolate and corn syrup dissolve quickly enough and one is left with those stubborn fibers which lurk in the mouth and, eventually, maroon themselves in the crannies of one's teeth. The exceptions to this embargo are products in which the coconut is either toasted or combined with other crunchy ingredients, thus obscuring the cuticle effect. The example that comes to mind is the brash and ridiculous Chick-O-Stick, a wand of peanut butter encased in brittle and sprinkled with toasted coconut.

White chocolate: When I was eight or nine years old I flew from California to New York with my twin brother, Mike. We were unchaperoned and therefore doted on by the stewardesses, who snuck us each a special dessert from first class: a white chocolate lollipop. I wolfed mine down and, shortly thereafter, got violently ill. This was mortifying at the time. In retrospect, I'm sort of proud of myself. Vomiting strikes me as proper response to white chocolate, which is, in fact, *not* chocolate (as it contains no cocoa) but a scourge visited upon us by the inimical forces of Freak Evil.

2

CARAVELLE: AN ELEGY

Art arises from loss. I wish this weren't the case. I wish that every time I met a new woman and she rocked my world, I was inspired to write my ass off. But that is not what happens. What happens is we lie around in bed eating chocolate and screwing. Art is what happens when things don't work out, when you're licking your wounds. Art is, to a larger extent than people would like to think, a productive licking of the wounds.

Loss, after all, leads rather naturally to the quest. The Greeks want Helen. Odysseus wants to get home (eventually). Dante wants Beatrice. Ahab wants the whale. Proust wants his cookies. And so on.

In the instant case, this entire book arose from the loss of a single candy bar. I am speaking of the Caravelle, though for many years I had no name to attach to this want. I had only memories. I had myself, at the age of nine or so, anxious, bereft, on a bus downtown to meet the therapist assigned the dubious task of restoring my capacity for self-love, and I had Mac's Smoke Shop, where all the essential vices were gathered in the smoky, crepuscular gloom with men who were somehow lesser versions of my father, sad and preoccupied, right there next to me but totally out of reach, and where a glorious central rack of candy, which was, in turn, gathered around this one candy bar in its bright yellow wrapper. It cost a quarter. There were two pieces per pack.

What was the Caravelle? It was a strip of caramel covered in a thick shell of milk chocolate, which was embedded with crisped rice. Yes, I know. That's the 100 Grand. But no one with even the dullest palate could ever have confused the two. The chocolate in the 100 Grand is mild and crumbly. The crisped rice is mealy and deflated. The caramel is the color of a washed-out varnish. And the balance is all wrong. There simply isn't enough chocolate or crisped rice to sustain the salivary breakdown. As a result, you wind up with a mouthful of rubbery caramel.

The Caravelle tasted more like a pastry: the chocolate was thicker, darker, full-bodied, and the crisped rise had a malty flavor and what I want to call structural integrity; the caramel was that rarest variety, dark and lustrous and supple, with hints of fudge. More so, there was a sense of the piece *yielding* to the mouth. By which I mean, one had to work the teeth through the sturdy chocolate shell, which gave way with a distinct, moist snap, through the crisped rice (thus releasing a second, grainy bouquet), and only then into the soft caramel core. Oh, that inimitable combination of textures! That symphony of flavors! And how they offered themselves to the heat and wetness of the mouth—the sensation of the crisped rice drenched in melted chocolate, chomped by the molars into the creamy swirl of caramel. Oh, woe and pity unto thee who never tasted this bar! True woe! True pity!

Around the time I was starting high school, Cadbury acquired Peter Paul and the Caravelle was discontinued. I didn't know this, of course. All I knew was that the best candy bar in the world was *gone*. And I went looking for the Caravelle everywhere. After a while, I couldn't even remember the name of the bar, which meant that I spent countless hours describing it to one or another bemused shopkeeper, girlfriend, therapist. Strangers at parties. Potential muggers. I was frantic, inconsolable, *really* annoying.

The disappearance of the Caravelle led me to the larger question: How is it that a candy bar, an absolutely sensational candy bar, can be banished to oblivion? How can the lovers of caramel and chocolate and crisped rice be left to satisfy themselves with the mealy indelicacy of the 100 Grand? This was an outrage, on par with VHS crushing Beta, a clear-cut consumer injustice perpetrated by that wonderful open market we're all so careful to abide.

It should be clear, at this point, that I'm more or less out of my mind. But so are you. Because every one of you has some form of the Freak within you, has sought the succor of sweets in a moment of trauma, has attached some sacred set of memories to the small, attainable pleasures of candy. Because everyone, as a child, had the same basic wiring and that wiring ran directly from the id to the freak to the memory bank, because our most cogent memory triggers—our senses of smell and taste—are the ones most closely associated with the experience of the world in our mouths.

And this is why, when I bring up candy at a party or to a colleague or to the guy who comes to check the gas meter, there is this immediate outpouring of memories, confessions, opinions, regrets, which doesn't happen when I bring up other hobbies of mine, such as bridge.

A few years ago, my friends began urging me to write a book about candy. Their reasoning ran as follows: Maybe if Steve *writes* about candy, he will *shut up* about candy. I didn't listen to these suggestions, of course, because I'm fairly stubborn and because, at the time, I considered candy to be a subject unworthy of my artistic consideration, meaning that I might actually enjoy writing such a book and thus automatically violate the serious young writer's credo: *Suffer at all times, preferably in such a manner as to convey to the rest of the world just how much you're suffering.* So I went about my business of suffering, flamboyantly, with much deep-hearted kvetching to the proper maternal surrogates.

A couple of years ago, though, I was driving down Massachusetts Avenue and I noticed, for perhaps the 500th time, the giant chimney atop the New England Confectionery Company, which is painted in the style of a giant package of Necco wafers, and I thought of my dear old pop and his ancient Necco jones and, well, I didn't do anything.

But then, a week later, I was driving through east Cambridge and I saw this run-down factory with a sign painted on the side that read SQUIRREL NUT BRAND. This was a terribly sad sight, because, though the place was all chipped brick and broken windows, the lettering itself was bright and hopeful. It reminded me of the giant red Schrafft's sign that still lords over Charlestown and how, years ago, Schrafft's had been the big kahuna of the boxed chocolates world, and how the sign is just a curiosity today, a little local color affixed to the top of a building filled with software companies. It began to dawn on me, in other words, that Boston, my adopted city, had something of an untold freak history.

When I called Squirrel Nut to find out what had happened, a friendly man named Bob Stengal answered the phone. He explained that he had been the general manager of Squirrel Nut Brands since 1970, but that he no longer served in that capacity because the company had been bought out and relocated to Texas, of all places, and though he wished the new owners the best of luck, you could tell that the whole scenario bummed him out.

The Squirrel Nut Zippers are perhaps best known these days as a band that played neoflapper music, music I spent several years trying quite hard (and never quite successfully) to enjoy. The original Squirrel Nut Zipper is a caramel nut chew, which has been in production since 1888. "We made one of the best taffies in the industry," Bob told me. "It chewed beautifully. A good taffy should be soft enough to pull without snapping. Why, you could pull ours forever."

I myself could attest to this. I had eaten several thousand Nut Zippers, because my optometrist stocked them in his candy bowl, meaning I ate twelve to fifteen during the course of an average visit, more if he had to replace my nose pads.

Before signing on with Squirrel Nut, Bob had been a shortening salesman, an occupation I hadn't realized existed previous to our discussion, but which, nonetheless, lent him a rather intimate acquaintance with the city's candyscape. Back in the fifties, he told me, four factories had operated near the old Coast Guard station, off Atlantic Avenue downtown—Royal, Cole, Haviland, and Liberty—pumping the smell of chocolate over the North End all day long. Main Street in Cambridge was known as Confectioner's Row. The entire street was candy makers: James O. Welch (Junior Mints), Jack Smiley (hard candies), Graylock Confection (Tweet), Dagget (chocolates), Fox-Cross (Charleston Chew). One by one, these companies fell on hard times. The managers would call Stengal to discuss their problems. Should they sell out? Should they relocate? Pretty soon Squirrel Nut was the last independent, family-owned candy company in Boston.

I decided to visit Bob at his home, in Concord. He was a trim fellow, with neatly cropped white hair and a sweet, rabbity face. He showed me a bunch of memorabilia from his years with the company: awards, pictures of him with the owners, trade show programs going yellow at the edges. "I guess I was in denial right until they moved," Bob said. "I didn't empty my desk until two weeks before they shut the place down. By the end, I didn't even *have* a desk. I was balancing a pad on my knee to take notes. They'd shut the utilities off, so it was dark. I remember I went up to the fourth floor of the factory and there was this echo. All the machines were gone. And I realized: this is just a shell now. Because, you know, when the factory was running, every floor had its own sounds. And when you were on the first floor, you could hear them all together, all those machines and people. It was like an orchestra."

You don't have to be a genius to see how a guy like Bob might shake me up. All that freak, all that loss.

But what I really needed was what little Charlie Bucket needed: to get myself inside a factory. I called over to Necco and got patched through to Walter Marshall, Vice President of Corporate Planning/Logistics, which translates as the Guy Who Has to Deal with All the Media Hassles, of whom I was hardly the most pressing. On the day I visited him, Marshall was anticipating a visit from Martha Stewart, the prescandal Martha, who wanted to talk with him about what had become Necco's most popular product, the Conversation Heart.

These are the little colored hearts that flood the market at Valentine's and carry messages such as KISS ME and LOVER BOY. Every year, Necco organized a ceremony at which Marshall—who was, in a promotional flourish exquisitely unsuited to his laconic demeanor, known as the King of Hearts—unveiled a new slogan. (This was Necco's effort to keep up with the times, and while I could appreciate the bid for free publicity, some of the more recent efforts had been less than titillating—FAX ME, for example.)

Marshall was in a tizzy. He was wearing a lab coat with his name stitched above the breast pocket and a tie knotted a bit too tightly, and the lab coat fluttered behind him as he whisked around the corporate offices of Necco. He settled behind his desk, a desk littered with candy hearts and memos regarding candy hearts, and fixed me with a look of not-quite-concealed impatience. "Alright, here's the story of how I got into the candy business," he said, though I had not yet asked him how he got into the candy business.

Marshall's father, it turned out, had been a traffic cop in front of the Schrafft's building. So Marshall landed himself a summer job in 1953 and stayed with the company for 25 years, working his way up to Executive Vice President/General Manager. He joined Necco in 1987 and was now, he reported, "in the twilight of a mediocre career." I found this odd. Here was a man who could take an elevator down one flight and order an entire run of chocolate-covered turtles and take them home with him. This did not strike me as the prerogative of a mediocre career.

Whatever his self-esteem issues, Marshall possessed an encyclopedic knowledge of the city's confectionery past, which began in 1765, when an Irish immigrant named John Hannon established America's first chocolate mill on the banks of the Neponset River in Dorchester. Marshall himself was born in Dorchester and used to walk by that factory every day. "You could almost taste the chocolate in the air," he said. The earliest candy companies in Boston were roadside operations. They cooked stuff up in the kitchen and sold it out front. The proximity of the chocolate mill, two sugar refineries, not to mention a sizable population, made the city a confectionery hub. With the introduction of the steam engine, local companies began producing the first candy-making machines. Foremost among these was Oliver R. Chase's lozenge cutter, which began producing the wafers later known as Neccos in 1847. They were a staple of the Union soldiers who fought in the Civil War. In 1901, Chase bought two other companies and dubbed his outfit the New England Confectionery Company, the world's first candy conglomerate.

The first half of the twentieth century was, Marshall assured me, Boston's freak zenith. The city was home to 140 candy companies by 1950, with sales of $200 million per year. Necco's Sky Bar—a slab of milk chocolate infused with four distinct fillings—was among the most popular bars on the East Coast. When World War II ended, all the New York papers ran stories reporting that the famous Sky Bar billboard in Times Square was finally illuminated again.

The beginning of the end for Boston came with the rise of the national candy conglomerates: Hershey's and Mars. They understood that distribution had changed. Mom-and-pop stores were on the wane. Manufacturers had to connect with the big chains. And they had to be more centrally located, so they could ship nationwide.

Unable to compete with the candy giants, Necco flirted with insolvency during the sixties. The company's execs realized they were going to have to grow to survive and began buying up struggling competitors. There was no shortage: Candy House Buttons, maker of those curious strips of colored candy dots on wax paper. Stark, Necco's only competitor in the wafer and candy heart world, and producers of the old-school peanut butter taffy known as the Mary Jane. Great American Brands, best known for its Haviland chocolates. And, just last year, the venerable Clark Bar Company of Pittsburgh. What Necco had amassed, not entirely on purpose, was a retro candy empire.

Marshall looked up from his desk. He was done with his lecture. Martha Stewart was, presumably, waiting in the wings. (FAX ME!) The moment of truth had now arrived.

"I'd like to tour the factory," I said.

Marshall sighed. "Fine. We can have Manny show you around."

I ♥ MANNY

Manny De Costa, the facilities manager at Necco, met me the next day at company headquarters on Mass Ave. He looked like a slightly puffed version of Norman Schwarzkopf: stern, firm-chinned, capable of inflicting significant damage with his bare hands, though he turned out to be the nicest man imaginable and no danger to anyone at all, unless you happened to be coated in chocolate.

The retro theme of Necco extended to the decor, which could have been generously described as Late Eisenhower. The elevator had a gold-plated dial above it, with an arrow to indicate the floor. The filing cabinets were wooden. On the wall was a poster, illustrated in the manner of a *Watchtower* magazine, which read NECCO: THE MODERN CANDIES WITH A TRADITION OF QUALITY. The only indication that the Korean War had, in fact, ended was the 'N Sync poster in the receptionist's cage.

"This building's been here since 1927, so a lot of this stuff is from quite a while ago," Manny explained. "We don't really throw anything out." Manny himself had come to Necco as a shipping clerk 35 years ago. (His father had been an elevator operator.) Now, Manny oversaw six floors and 400 employees. He was dressed in a suit and tie, which he accented—for our visit to production areas—with a white gauzy shower cap that sat on his head like a collapsed soufflé.

The secret to virtually all nonchocolate candy, Manny explained, was time and temperature. The longer and higher you cooked the basic ingredients—sugar, corn syrup, starch—the harder the candy became. On the fifth floor, where Necco made taffy, they were heating the staples to 243 degrees in gigantic kettles. The taffy was then poured onto cooling wheels the size of steamrollers, which squeezed the stuff into sheets that looked like stained glass. The taffy, still a blazing 180 degrees, was cut into 67-pound batches and heaved onto cooling tables, then lugged onto mechanical pulling hooks.

The taffy, yanked to and fro by two rotating arms, gradually softened and turned opaque. At this point, the glob—looking very much like an albino python—got hoisted onto the batch roller, a pair of knobbed rotating wheels which massaged the taffy into a thin rope. The next machine chopped the rope into bite-size pieces, wrapped them in waxed paper, and sent them whizzing down a conveyor belt for packing. Manny plucked a piece off the belt and handed it to me. It was still warm.

Down on the third floor, wafer production was in full swing and I immediately experienced that overwhelming olfactory blast known as Halloween Smell; a free-floating bouquet of sugar, cocoa butter, and flavorings. The wafers required no boiling. Instead, the ingredients were pulverized in giant mixers, producing a grainy paste that looked sort of like caviar, if you can envision caviar in the neon register. The paste was rolled into thin sheets and punched into the desired shape. This punching happened very quickly. (So quickly that it occurred to me—in one of those moments of morbid speculation that besets me when I'm overstimulated—that I could have slipped my hand under one of the mechanized pistons and wound up with Necco stigmata.) At peak efficiency, a single assembly line can kick out 38,000 pounds of candy per day, or 15,390,000 wafers. I am not going to tell you that this is enough wafers to stretch from the earth to the moon six times. I will say, only, that it is *a lot of fucking wafers*.

Manny, who displayed an endearing (if not entirely hygienic) habit of sampling the raw paste for quality with his thumb, was a lifelong fan. "We used to go to the movie theater and fling them at the screen. Actually, we only threw the ones we didn't like. I didn't like the purple ones, so I threw those." Anyone familiar with the Necco flavor pantheon will commend Manny on his good taste in this matter. I myself had often pondered just what flavor purple was supposed to signify. Frankincense? Turpentine? The correct answer, as Manny noted with some dismay, was *clove*. Why anyone would wish to produce a clove-flavored candy remained obscure. (Paging MWM.)

The Necco packing process had changed very little over the years. Tubs of wafers were fed into a giant hopper and poured down a pipe from the third floor to the second, where they funneled into rows. A crew of women then pinched up a length of wafers between their two index fingers and dropped them in racks. Picture having to fill roll after roll of quarters in a faint cloud of sugared starch, and you get the idea. The racks were pushed along to a final inspector, who surveyed each package to make sure all eight colors were represented among the 38 to 40 wafers per pack. If not, she plucked out repeats and inserted missing colors. All this happened in approximately four seconds. The floor beneath this operation was a vast and dazzling fresco of broken wafers.

The big buzz around Necco was the company's newest acquisition, the Clark Bar. With good reason. It is possible to say that you have not lived a fully actualized life unless you have eaten a Clark Bar straight off the assembly line. I am qualified to make this judgment because I have eaten a Clark Bar straight off the assembly line. I have eaten two.

A native of Pittsburgh, the Clark was first produced in 1917 and became one of the most popular bars of the post–World War II candy boom. It consists of a crunchy peanut filling covered in a milk chocolate coating. Most people would compare it to the Butterfinger, though it has far more peanut flavor than a Butterfinger and a softer bite. Necco itself used to produce a chocolate-covered peanut crunch known as the Bolster Bar. But everyone seemed to agree the Clark Bar was tastier. This, according to Manny, is because of the Clark's unique production process.

> Step 1: The staples were boiled into a sticky glop, cooled, and pulled to a beige, taffylike consistency.
>
> Step 2: The filling was fed into a huge machine which

flattened it and spread a layer of real peanut butter on top. A single worker, hovering over the machine with a spatula, rolled this slab into a sort of giant burrito. This step was the linchpin of the entire Clark gestalt. It ensured that the filling was striated into sediments of peanut butter and crunch. (Manny later demonstrated this to me by biting a snack-size bar lengthwise and showing me the sediments.)

Step 3: The burrito was lowered into a batch roller, where it was funneled down and came snaking out, ticker-tape style, to be cut into segments.

Step 4: The peanut crunch was now ready to be covered in chocolate, a process known as enrobing. Enrobing is the money shot of candy production, a sight so sensual as to seem pornographic. The conveyor belt carried the naked Clarks forward, into a curtain of chocolate, which, in spilling down, created the delicate ripples and wavelets you find atop most candy bars. It is this illusion of liquidity that I have always found so seductive; when we look at the top of a candy bar, what we see is a particular moment, the dynamism of the fluid state captured.

Step 5: The wet bars were carried into a cooling tunnel. A half hour later they emerged, 100 yards down the line, ready for packing. The entire genesis of the Clark, from raw ingredients to wrapper, took 90 minutes.

The fresh bar had a more supple consistency than store-bought. The peanut butter was more redolent. The chocolate coating melted the moment it hit your tongue. "Fresh off the line is a different thing," Manny said. "It's like from someone's kitchen. I eat them all day long. That's why I'm as big as I am."

It was precisely at this moment, watching Manny De Costa pat his stomach and laugh in a jolly vibrato while offering me a second fresh Clark Bar, that I considered asking him to adopt me. This feeling was reinforced during our brief trip to the sample shop on the first floor, where Manny and his wife—who, it turned out, worked in the sample shop and was, if this is even possible, *nicer* than Manny—foisted a shameful amount of candy onto me, which I tried (not very hard) to refuse, and which I seriously considered donating to orphans, before deciding, instead, to eat it all myself.

FEEDING THE BEAST

That was my first taste of industrial candy production. I was delirious. I called Walter Marshall and explained, as calmly as I could, that I would need to tour the Haviland factory as well. Marshall acceded, without much enthusiasm.

I arrived at the factory only to find a huge tanker truck parked out front, the kind commonly used to transport gas or heating oil. In this case, it was transporting corn syrup. The syrup was pumped into the building through an industrial-sized fire hose, which was screwed into a valve in the side of the building—the corn syrup valve. It was labeled. This pleased me inordinately, as did the lobby and the stairwells and the elevator, all of which smelled like chocolate. (Is it humanly possible to dislike a facility in which the elevators smell like chocolate?)

The factory itself was on its last legs. The machines were aging. The production floors were cramped and awkwardly laid out. Plastic tarps had been hastily affixed to certain areas of the ceiling, to contain leaks. The fellow assigned to show me around, a young engineer named Eric Saborin, was unfazed by these problems. Short of something landing on his actual head, he was not going to sweat a little clutter.

The majority of the Haviland factory was composed of assembly lines, virtually all of which were dedicated to coating something in chocolate: caramel squares, raspberry jellies, coconut creams. On one floor, a machine plinked out soft kisses of chocolate, then sprinkled them with tiny white beads of sugar, to create nonpareils. Nearby, I watched row after row of peppermint disks enrobed in dark chocolate—the vaunted Haviland Thin Mints (HTM).

A few words about this ferociously underrated product: The standard HTM has a chocolate-to-mint ratio of greater than 50 percent. If, like me, you buy seconds, you can often find mutant batches in which the chocolate layers have come out even thicker. A fresh HTM has an almost liquid center and a mint flavor that is mild enough to complement the chocolate, rather than overwhelming it. Even at retail prices, one can buy a five-ounce box for a buck. In short, the HTM makes the York Peppermint Pattie its bitch.

Saborin was busy explaining to me "the volatile nature of the chocolate medium." You couldn't just melt chocolate down and start pouring. Oh no. It had to be prepped in special kettles, heated, cooled, then heated again, a process called tempering. A piece of chocolate that had been properly tempered had a beautiful sheen, almost like glass. "It should snap," Saborin explained. He picked up an HTM and snapped it in two. Then, without a word of warning, he threw both halves into a trash bin.

This happened so quickly I didn't know quite what to do. I stood there in a little cloud of disillusionment. Saborin had somehow become inured to the holiness of his work product and this struck me as a very distressing situation indeed, given that I'm someone who has been known to eat the pieces of candy found underneath my couch.

Haviland's most intriguing area was the panning room, which consisted of two rows of squat copper urns, known as . . . pans. The panning technique originated in Italy, well before the rise of industrial machines. Basically, you threw a bunch of peanuts, or raisins, inside the pan, poured in a liquid sugar coating, and started spinning. The constant circular motion ensured that each piece was evenly coated.

Modern panning technology is a bit more sophisticated. At Haviland, the panning staff—covered head-to-toe in white, like the workers at a nuclear reactor—used special nozzles to spray chocolate onto the rotating morsels. They were also able to adjust cold-air vents to keep pieces from sticking together. On the day I visited, the panners were in full Easter frenzy. More than a dozen nozzles were going and the air in the panning room was permeated with chocolate vapor. I was breathing *chocolate air*.

Saborin took me into the adjoining storage room to show me the finished product: malted milk eggs. Trays of them were stacked, one atop the next, to keep the lovely speckled shells from fading in the light. Saborin reached into a bin, pulled out a purple egg, and bit it in half, so I could see the multiple layers: the malted center, the chocolate coating, the speckled candy shell, and the shellac. I doubt Saborin envisioned, back when he was getting his degree in mechanical engineering, that he would someday explain the technical intricacies of his job by biting into a malted milk egg. But he seemed perfectly happy and asked me if I wanted to go downstairs to see the chocolate bunnies.

These were, in point of fact, marshmallow bunnies covered

in chocolate. They rode the conveyor belt three astride, looking nonchalant in profile, as a curtain of milk chocolate washed down onto their white fleshy pelts and enveloped them and seeped off to reveal the dimensions of their bodies in a lustrous brown. Saborin was saying something or other, involving, I think, starch. I was watching the bunnies.

Simply: I could not stop watching the bunnies, the way the light struck the wet chocolate from above, the creamy falling away of the excess into a darkened pool below, the steel machinery flecked and streaked in brown. The workers overseeing the production line didn't seem to know what to do. I myself didn't know what to do. I was obviously experiencing some kind of dramatic psychic event, one that bordered on the disassociative. I had fallen into what I would later come to recognize as a freaktrance, a state of involuntary rapture induced by watching candy production at close range. These trances were the result of several factors.

First, the presence of huge, precisely calibrated machinery just *made me hot*. This has to do with my own mechanical ineptitude, which is of a degree that I recently spent two and a half hours attempting to replace my windshield wipers. For me, the chance to watch a mechanical process—the flawless execution of a series of intricate actions, the stainless steel ingenuity of it all—was deeply reassuring. It restored my faith in physics, a discipline I have never quite understood, despite having taken an Advanced Placement course senior year in high school. Most humans share this fascination, because we are, by our nature, messy, flawed, inconsistent, conflicted. Mass production is the opposite of all these things.

We are, furthermore, in the midst of what I would call a *radical object disconnect*. For most of human history, people essentially knew where their stuff came from. The farmer grew your carrots. The tailor stitched your britches. The cobbler made your shoes. But as the world has become industrialized, people have drifted away from the means of production. Technology is out there, somewhere, banging out our products in ever more sophisticated manners, and they show up brightly wrapped in our vast emporiums and we pay for them with plastic cards. Watching the process by which our products are made reconnects us to the wonders of production. Indeed, it provides a soothing sense of technology as our benefactor, in a naïve every-day-in-every-way-we-are-getting-better-and-better kind of way.

The candy factory, in particular, places all the foul props of the modern age in the service of our most innocent desires. To watch huge, metal machines plink out delicate chocolate bunnies—what delicious irony! The bogeyman of technology tamed! Bunnies not bombs! This is a bunch of crapola, of course. Candy companies are servants of late-model capitalism, just as surely as Exxon and Dow. They dehumanize workers, both here and abroad, and pump out pollution and provide an indulgence that is unconscionable, given the great many people on the planet who are starving to death—which is all the more reason to lose oneself in the trance. In the trance, all that matters is the thing before you: the sheen of the chocolate, the tumble of peanuts, the dappled river of caramel, the miraculous union of these parts into a whole.

At a certain point, Saborin realized I'd fallen under the chocolate spell. He came and gently touched my elbow. "You okay?"

I nodded, a little dizzily. "It's just so lovely."

"Wait till next year," he said. "We're moving to a new factory over in Revere. All new machines. It'll make this place look like the Stone Age."

3

A TOP-SECRET CHOCOLATE SITUATION

I was pretty fired up now, as it had become clear to me that actual professionals in the candy industry would grant me access to actual candy factories. So I decided to call Tootsie Roll Industries, the Chicago-based company that owns Cambridge Brands, Boston's other major candy concern. Its factory, the last remaining on Confectioner's Row, produced Junior Mints, Sugar Babies, and Charleston Chews.

I explained to Ellen Gordon, the president, that I was a huge fan of Tootsie Rolls and Tootsie Pops, that I had done some major bonding with my dad over Junior Mints, that I had frozen approximately 243 Strawberry Charleston Chews over the years and cracked each and every one of them on the kitchen counter of our old house on Wilkie Way, that it was very likely microscopic shards of said product which accounted for the chronic ant problem we experienced during my middle school years, and that given all this I would be more than happy to tour the Cambridge Brands plant at her convenience.

Ms. Gordon laughed politely and explained that no such visit would be possible. For competitive reasons, she said, not impolitely. She assured me that the manufacturing process for the products in question was proprietary and that the company's equipment was beyond state of the art.

"Beyond state of the art," I said. "Surely you jest. Junior Mints enrobed with lasers? Genetically engineered Sugar Babies?"

"Sorry," Gordon said.

As it turns out, the larger candy manufacturers are notoriously secretive operations. I had always assumed that the industrial espionage in *Charlie and the Chocolate Factory* was trumped-up fiction. Not so. Roald Dahl based his book on the legendary exploits of the Cadburys and Rowntrees, who routinely sent moles to spy on one another's operations.

A young Forrest Mars, the founder of Mars (which now goes by the yummy-sounding name Masterfoods, and which I will continue to refer to as Mars, both out of antiglobalist zeal and basic kindness to the reader), briefly worked in a Swiss chocolate factory, for the express purpose of sussing out trade secrets. His chief competitor, Milton S. Hershey, reportedly toured various Swiss factories during the era when he was trying to learn how to make milk chocolate.

There are three reasons that espionage remains such a big anxiety in the candy industry:

1. You can't patent a chocolate bar. You can patent a name and a wrapper and a logo. But the recipes and ingredients are fair game; there is nothing to stop a competitor from selling a copycat version of your product. Hershey's Skor Bar, for instance, was a bald-faced attempt to win the chocolate-covered-butter-toffee market from the Heath bar. (Hershey's eventually wound up purchasing Heath, thus ensuring a total monopoly.)
2. The staple ingredients of most candies are quite similar, which means that the vital data resides in the manufacturing process.
3. Success, in the candy market, often has less to do with producing the best candy as with getting to market first. When a candy company comes up with a popular innovation—such as the production of a snack-size bar—the competition had better figure out how to match the feat, and quickly.

I spoke to Joël Glenn Brenner about all this, because she was probably better qualified than anyone to discuss the paranoia that pervades the candy industry. Several years ago, she published a terrific book called *The Emperors of Chocolate*, which detailed the vicious historical competition between

Mars and Hershey. As a reporter for the *Wall Street Journal,* Brenner spent years attempting to gain access to the Mars plant, a process she described as "pretty miserable. It's just a terribly closed environment."

And not just to nosy reporters. As Brenner observed in her book, outside workers called in to repair machinery in areas considered proprietary are blindfolded, allowed to fix the machine in question, then blindfolded and escorted out of the plant. Hershey's isn't much better. The company may try to project a fuzzy, all-American image, but we're talking about an operation that *shreds its marketing plans.*

On the other hand, Brenner said, the secrecy is necessary to some extent. There are secrets in the industry worth millions, and the only way to get them is to get inside the plant, or to pay someone to get inside. "Look at the Wonderball fiasco," Brenner said. The Wonderball is a Nestlé product, basically a milk chocolate ball with hard candies inside. There were a couple of companies that wanted to introduce the same kind of product in America, and the result was a frenzy of spying, or alleged spying, amongst the larger candy companies. This happened all of three years ago. The competition to get to market is that fierce. In a tone of undisguised relief, Brenner told me that she no longer covered the candy industry. But the trend in candy was the same as elsewhere, she assured me, "The big guys gobble up the little guys or drive them out of business." This has resulted in an industry that operates on two distinct planes:

1. The Big Three (Nestlé, Hershey's, Mars); and
2. All the other little freaks.

Nestlé was launched 125 years ago by the milk chocolate pioneer Henri Nestlé. In recent years, the Swiss company has become a multinational behemoth, snapping up the British chocolate giant Rowntree, the Italian Perugina, Baby Ruth, Butterfinger, Oh Henry! and a dozen other brands.

Most Americans had never even heard of chocolate in 1893, when Milton S. Hershey attended the Columbian Exposition in Chicago. (The question that leaps to mind here, rather stubbornly, is why on earth they would want to go on living, but I will leave that aside for now.) Hershey himself made caramels, but the moment he saw and smelled the exhibit devoted to producing chocolate bars he knew he was witnessing the freak of the future and snapped up the entire operation. He spent a decade figuring out how to mass-produce milk chocolate bars and, just as important, sold them in previously unheard-of venues—groceries, pharmacies, diners. The empire has expanded to include Reese's Peanut Butter Cups, Milk Duds, Almond Joy, Heath, Whatchamacallit, and some dozen other bars. (Fun fact: The *S* stands for Snavely.)

Forrest Mars went through his share of failures as a

confectioner—among his numerous flops was a pineapple-flavored Mars bar—but by the forties he had established himself as Hershey's chief competitor. Shrewd, abstemious, and famously publicity shy, Mars was the first man to recognize the global reach of the candy bar market. Among the company's gazillion products are Milky Way, M&M's, and the most popular candy bar in America, Snickers.

THE POLITICS OF THE RACK

All this is worth noting, in a *Wall Street Journal*ish sort of way. But it was the second group, the little guys, that intrigued me. In my own pathologically romantic sense of things, I viewed these companies as throwbacks to the bygone era of candy, when each town had its own individual brands. And the good peoples of this country would gather together in public squares with lots of trees and perhaps a fellow picking a banjo, and they would partake of the particular candy bar produced in their town and feel a surge of sucrose-fueled civic identity. What I really wanted to do was to visit these companies—if any still existed—and to chronicle their struggles for survival in this wicked age of homogeneity, and, not incidentally, to load up on free candy.

But I needed a source still in the business. I turned to Lisbeth Echeandia, the former publisher of *Confectioner Maga-*

zine. Echeandia, now a candy consultant, lives in Texas and is married to a Spaniard but is, in fact, confusingly, Australian. She thought my idea was just lovely, maybe even historically vital, given that so many smaller candy companies were going belly-up. The industry would eventually consist of 150 companies, she predicted, down from the 6,000 concerns that thrived during the boom years between the World Wars. This was not a particularly controversial forecast in the candy world. Echeandia was also a champion of the small, independent candy companies. "It's so tough for them to survive," she said, "with these slotting fees."

"What's a slotting fee?" I said.

"If you want your product on the racks," she explained, "you have to pay a slotting fee. And they can be very expensive."

"Wait a second," I said. "You mean companies have to *pay* to get their stuff into stores?"

Yup.

Echeandia explained that the larger retail chains charge tens of thousands of dollars to place a particular candy bar in the racks near the register. Very few people, after all, head into the supermarket with Twix on their shopping list. Instead, they get stuck in the checkout line and the candy rack starts to call out to them, sirenlike, and they take a look at the wrappers and get a freakbuzz, accompanied, invariably, by the Guilt Hammer, which strikes them just behind the left ear. And if you watch people carefully around these racks—as I do—you can see this terrible internal struggle played out: the sideways glance at the wrappers, the contrite straightening up, the useless effort to lose oneself in the gossip rags (BEN EATS J-LO'S ASS IN BLOODY CANNIBAL FEAST!) followed by a second, lingering inspection, during which the consumer is, in fact, fantasizing about the various candy bars, imagining them naked, conjuring up that first, illicit bite, followed sometimes by a soft fingering of the wrapper, and, in most cases, a furious snatch of the desired bar, to be buried beneath the healthiest item in the basket. Oh woe to us so staggered by our self-love!

If there's a child involved, this conflict is neatly externalized. He or she plays the role of tyrannical id, while the adult, usually a mother already worn down by the rigors of guiding a tyrannical id through fourteen aisles, offers token resistance. (Note that the average height of most candy racks corresponds directly to the height of a child.) During a visit to my local market, I heard the following exchange between a girl of about eight and her father.

GIRL: Does everyone die?
DAD: You're not going to die for a long time, honey.
GIRL: But everyone does die, right?
DAD: Not for a long, long time.

GIRL: Maddy told me everyone dies.

DAD: Maddy (inaudible).

GIRL: Aren't you afraid to die, Dad?

DAD: You know what, sweetie? You shouldn't worry about things like that. You know what you should worry about? Just being alive and being happy.

GIRL: (pause) Dad, can we get Hershey's Kisses?

Obviously, those companies without the financial resources to afford slotting fees are at a huge disadvantage. They can't get stocked at the major chain supermarkets or convenience stores or pharmacies. They have to make do at the smaller, independent outlets—which are themselves being driven out of business—or at discount stores.

This is just business. Retailers want things as simple and profitable as possible. If stores can deal with a half-dozen companies and fill their racks and get paid, why should they bother with a smaller candy company that makes only one product? The problem with this logic, Echeandia observed, is that candy isn't like other products. There's no great advantage to stocking, say, a huge variety of laundry soaps, because consumers view this product as an impersonal necessity. But with candy, the buy impulse is intimate and discretionary, most often triggered by the very sight of a particular piece. More variety means more triggers. And the longer you keep a consumer in front of the racks, the more triggers you hit. I myself have always been unreasonably drawn to candy suppliers with an abundant rack (such as the Old Barrel) for this very reason.

But the racks are just a means to an end, which is to achieve hegemony over the average American mouth. Tastes are not inborn, after all. They are developed. The reason Americans favor milk chocolate over dark is because Milton Hershey got his bars into enough American mouths to establish our collective taste. His interest was not in establishing variety, but just the opposite. He wanted everyone eating the same bar—his.

Given this paradigm, it became clear why the candy giants were so eager to establish beachheads in China, the former Soviet Union, and the developing world. Advertising and marketing campaigns can go a long way toward selling tennis shoes. But with candy bars, it's all about the intimate experience of the product in a person's mouth, because eventually the tastes and textures of that experience—the creaminess of the chocolate, the crunch of the peanuts, the elasticity of the caramel—take up residence in the sense memory. This is why most people can conjure up, so precisely, the experience of eating their favorite candy bar. In the common parlance this is called a craving.

The Big Three were locked in an economic battle with billions of dollars at stake, Echeandia explained. So naturally, they'd tried to become all things to all people. They never used to make seasonal pieces. That niche was left to smaller companies. Now they all made special pieces for the holidays. When you ate a Milky Way in Christmas foil, you were actually reinforcing the desire for that brand. They also had attempted to provide variety by continually introducing new bars. Most of these were actually brand extensions, the confectionary equivalent to Hollywood sequels: Reese's Peanut Butter Sticks, M&M's Crispy, and so on. To cite a particularly blatant recent example: Mars recently phased out its namesake bar and replaced it with the Snickers Almond, a nearly identical bar, in the hopes of cashing in on its hottest brand name.

Consolidation had not been limited to the merchandising side. Many of the larger distributors would no longer carry candy that didn't sell to the major chains. This was crucial for smaller companies, which often couldn't afford their own fleet of refrigerated trucks and storage spaces, meaning they couldn't ship their products when the weather got too warm. The Big Three, by contrast, had built their own distribution systems. As Brenner detailed in her book, Mars had established dominance in the Arab world by building refrigerated distribution centers and in-store displays.

The Big Three were also at a huge advantage when it came to securing raw materials. Both Hershey's and Mars, for instance, owned cocoa plantations. They made their own chocolate, selling the surplus to smaller companies. They had enough buying power to minimize the fluctuations of the commodities market. Thanks to the political muscle of domestic sugar producers, for instance, American sugar prices were being kept artificially inflated. It had become cheaper to produce certain candies in Canada or Mexico and ship them back to the United States for sale.

Given the economic landscape, I wondered if any company, other than the Big Three, could ever introduce a new candy bar to the mainstream market?

Echeandia laughed. "There are easier ways to commit suicide," she said. "And it's a great pity, too, because people have an emotional relationship to candy. They get very shaken up if their favorite brand disappears." Echeandia herself used to travel to Canada to find childhood favorites such as the Crunchy Bar and the Violet Crumble.

THE LAST MAN IN AMERICA WITH BLACK JACK GUM

For further evidence, one needed look no further than the Internet, the last refuge of the obsessive, where a crop of companies had popped up to serve the emerging nostalgia candy market. The first and most prominent of these, CandyDirect.com, peddled a variety of sweets that had become hard to find retail. It was really a freak depot. This was most apparent on the site's message board, which was flooded with notes from folks desperately seeking some candy from their youth. I found myself deeply touched by these outbursts, which reassured me I was not alone in my freakdom. A few outtakes:

> *For the last 23 years or so I have had Malted Milk Eggs from Brach's. I need my Eggs. Where are they? I have looked in every drug store, every food store, and the local farmers market I can not find them anywhere. Please help with my withdralls* [sic]. *I think all the time about the egg in my mouth sucking the candy shell off then letting the chocolate melt in my mouth, then when it gets to the malted part you just let it dosolve* [*uh*, sic] *in your mouth.*

> *Well, I guess this is my last attempt!! I've tried to get any info regarding a gumball called "Zappers" No help from anyone. Last try!! Please help with even sharing just a memory.*

> *HELP ME, PLEASE!!!!!!!!!!!!! I NEED TO FIND ORANGE BUBBLE YUM BUBBLE GUM. NOT SHERBERT. ORANGE. I HAVE BEEN LOOKING FOR 2 YEARS. THIS IS MY BOYFRIENDS FAVORITE. IF I FIND IT HE MAY ASK ME TO MARRY HIM. IF YOU HAVE ANY INFO, PLEASE PLEASE CONTACT ME!!!!!*

CandyDirect.com was the brainchild of a fellow named Steve Traino, a 34-year-old native of Rochester, New York, and the most authentically American human being to whom I have ever spoken. I mean this as a compliment. He had wanted to be an entrepreneur his entire life. At age eight, he sold hand-drawn mazes to his classmates for a dime. Later, he ran a garage sale business, buying and reselling his neighbors' junk and splitting the profit with them. After graduating from college with a degree in business, he opened a frozen yogurt shop, which soon went under. He returned home to live with his parents and eventually drifted to San Diego, where he worked for Xerox and, later, for a couple of high-tech companies. He continued to harbor the dream of every conscientious American: to launch a business and become filthy rich.

Traino's decision to start CandyDirect.com was based on his stint as a Pop Rocks black marketeer back in the seventies. He, too, bought boxes of the candy in California and resold them at school. He even snagged the Poprocks.com domain name in 1996, though he never used it, fearing he'd get sued for copyright infringement. Instead, he broadened his scope to include all manner of rare candies.

"The hits were kind of slow at first," Traino recalled. "Luckily, I had a shower in the office."

"Wait a second," I said, "you had a shower in your office?"

"Actually, the shower was down the hall."

"So you lived in your office?"

"I tried to be kind of subtle about it, because I didn't want the landlords to find out. But they must have known. I mean, here I am, walking down the hall with my hair all wet." Traino chuckled softly. "I had a front part where the business was and a little room in back where I had my futon and a TV. I had satellite TV. It was right in Mission Valley, which is a really nice part of town. I used to go up on the roof and walk around at night. It was very peaceful. Then, as the business expanded, I graduated to an apartment, which doubled as an office, and then I graduated to an office *and* an apartment."

Traino, who had a friendly, somewhat scattered phone manner, told me a story about a young woman who came out from Michigan in search of an obscure fruit candy called Deltha Rolls. She sounded "you know, young and cute" on the phone, so Traino talked up the business and invited her to drop by the office. "I'm sure she thought it was going to be some huge warehouse. But it was just me, a guy living in his office."

Modesty notwithstanding, Traino was one of the first people to foresee the tremendous potential of the nostalgia candy market. Long before Ralph Lauren's daughter Dylan opened her candy boutique in Manhattan, Traino was peddling Deltha Rolls on-line. Today, he does about a million per year in sales and has four employees and a large air-conditioned facility for storage. One thing hasn't changed: his customers still tend to freak out when discussing their childhood candy passions. Occasionally, they weep. And they react with vehemence when manufacturers alter a recipe. A few months earlier, a Canadian company had bought out Fleer and made a slight change in the production of Double Bubble. Traino was bombarded with calls from customers desperate for the original formula.

Several years ago, he got a tip from some friends in the industry that Black Jack, a popular old-school licorice gum, was going to be discontinued. He spent half his savings buying up the available stock. "I had it all in my kitchen cupboards, because I was running the business out of my apartment at that point and I was sitting there looking at all this gum and I was scared to death. But I sold tons of that stuff, because I was the last person in the country to have Black Jack. It was the best investment I ever made."

This was a common situation for Traino. He had become, in this sense, a candy speculator, a last resort for the unrequited freak. He no longer even needed industry informants. He was able to figure out when a brand was going to be discontinued by the flood of calls from consumers unable to find it in stores.

At the same time, he was loathe to regard himself as a liquidator. He actually hated it when companies decided to drop a brand. He was furious when one of Nestlé's subsidiaries stopped making Wacky Wafers. "I talked to one of their product managers and he told me something about Wacky Wafers being too similar to Bottle Caps and how one line is cannibalizing the other line, something like that. This guy didn't even understand the difference between the products. Wacky Wafers are fruit-flavored. They're about the size of quarters. Bottle Caps are much smaller and they're flavored like sodas, which, I'm sorry, are not fruits. But you know what happens with these companies? They get a bunch of MBAs in there who've been working with computers and they don't care about candy. They're just in it to make a buck."

Traino had reached an interesting juncture in his moral logic. Because, after all, he too was in candy to make a buck. And yet, it was obvious he felt a true dedication to candy, that his product had become more than product to him. Traino had a hard time remaining indignant, though. He was too much of an optimist.

"What these companies should do," he decided, "Hershey's or one of the other big ones, they should buy up some of these smaller companies and start, like, a nostalgia line of candies. They could bring back the candies from the fifties and sixties and seventies. People love that stuff. What would be really cool is for candy to go the way that beer has, with all those microbrews that came in. Local candy bars could make a resurgence! That's one of my big plans, to get into manufacturing.

But you'd have to start small, with gift shops and word of mouth and the Internet."

Suddenly, Traino began to laugh. I began to laugh, as well. It was a wonderful thing to make your fortune selling candy. Wasn't America a wonderful country? I felt one of those rare bursts of faith, a sense of the world as a domain of wondrous good.

Almost immediately, a horrible thought occurred to me: Traino had probably voted for George W. Bush. He probably believed that America's role in the world economy was one of heroism, that the rest of the world—with its despots and starving masses and pathological martyrs—could be either rescued or rubbed out by good old American pluck, along with the proper inculcation of prevailing market theory. I thought about the news stories coming out of the Ivory Coast, where nearly half of the world's cocoa beans are grown, and where children are sold by their parents as slaves and sent into the cocoa plantations to work twelve hours a day, under conditions that the Western world would consider inhuman. Traino was still talking in eager, digressive gusts. He had big dreams and he wanted to send me a bag of Caramel M&M's and he wanted to know about the new Kit Kat Darks, which I'd mentioned to him earlier. But I was lost to him now, trapped in my own gloomy speculations.

I began to consider the history of candy, the ways in which

imperialism could be traced straight back to the gullet. The lust for sugar and spices was, after all, what drove the early explorers. And cocoa was, without a doubt, the most tragic import. Montezuma considered the beans a gift from the gods. He gave this gift to Cortés and Cortés brought it back to King Carlos of Spain and, within a few decades, half the courts of Europe were hooked. The Catholic Church regarded cocoa as so sacred that it was exempted from the prohibition of fasts. In more lascivious quarters, it was believed to boost sexual prowess (which only goes to show that chocolate has long been a legal sublimation of the erotic, something Cortés might have picked up from Montezuma, who throated a goblet nightly to brace himself for the sweet rigors of his harem). The demand for cocoa amongst the aristocracy was insatiable. And, because the fancy of the idle rich has always been the great unsung engine of progress, ships were quickly dispatched to the damp, humid regions of the globe to establish plantations and trade routes. In this way, the people of the Old World established dominion over the people of the New.

Fittingly, it was an American—the plucky Dutch immigrant Hershey—who produced bars for the masses. This had the effect of making chocolate seem egalitarian and carefree. But it was no surprise that the candy bar was popularized by the American soldiers of World War I, doughboys who traversed a conquered Europe with a rifle in one hand and a Hershey bar in the other. They were the conquistadors of our age, the advance force of late-model capitalism. Traino could dream all he wanted. (And I could cling to his optimism!) But the plantations were still out there, in the Ivory Coast, in Costa Rica, manned by starving children. Candy bars remained, in the end, the ultimate American palliative, a luxury paid for in blood but cheap enough to seem democratic.

I had friends, of course, who urged me to eat only selected chocolates, organically grown, on sustainable farms, by workers paid a decent wage. This was a totally reasonable compromise, and I meant to do so. But then the urge for pleasure would rise up and before I could stop myself I'd be licking the smooth underside of a Reese's Peanut Butter Cup. Never mind all the obedient liberal guilt. I was an addict, a confirmed freak, a willing accomplice of the modern imperial system, sweet-tongued and complicit.

4

THE CAPO DI TUTTI FREAK

Talking to Steve Traino was a curious experience. On the one hand, I found it comforting to know that someone out there was a bigger candyfreak than me. And, on the other, I felt that twinge of jealousy familiar to anyone who has spent several years privately gloating because they own the British import, only to discover there are people out there with the original demos—on four-track. I was, at best, a semipro. This became quite clear to me when I met Ray Broekel.

Broekel is a legend among the confectioniscienti, for the simple reason that he knows more about candy bars than anyone else on earth. He is the author of two books, *The Great American Candy Bar Book* (1982) and *The Chocolate Chronicles* (1985), both of which I would characterize, loosely, as illustrated history books. Virtually every person I'd spoken to about candy was aware of Broekel. A number of them were under the impression that he was deceased. He is not deceased, though he is, at 80, somewhat past his prime in terms of Olympic competition. Wonderfully enough, he lives in Ipswich, just an hour north of Boston. I called Broekel and told him I was a great fan of his work and that I wanted to visit him.

He paused for a long moment, breathing into the phone.

"Well, alright," he said.

Broekel's house is on a quiet street a few miles outside of town, just where the suburban streets give way to rural routes. He met me at the door, wearing a sweatshirt with Looney Tunes cartoon characters and a Chicago Cubs cap and large squarish glasses of the sort I associated with junior high school science teachers, which is what Broekel was before he became a full-time writer.

As on the phone, I began gushing about his work.

Broekel stood in the doorway, his eyebrows tipped skeptically, waiting for me to peter out. "Stuff's downstairs," he said and shuffled down to a sunken basement–type thing that I recognized immediately as the TV room of my childhood home: the same dispirited light and wood paneling and battered lampshades.

Or maybe it would be more accurate to say the room was what I fantasized our TV room might have looked like, had I been allowed to decorate. The shelves were jammed with candy boxes. I recognized a few (Mounds, Reggie!). But most were brands that predated me (Winkers, Toppers, I Scream, Pie Face, So Big, Cocoanut Cakes) with giddy fonts which had faded over the years.

One in particular that leapt out at me was Bit-O-Choc, because I'd just been explaining to my friend Ann that Bit-O-Honey did, in fact, produce a chocolate taffy bar for a few glorious years back in the seventies, a topic that enthralled me to no end. (Her response: "This topic is bit O boring.")

We stood there for a few minutes admiring the boxes.

"That's a lot of boxes," I said.

"There's more," he said.

He led me down the hall to an even smaller room, which was piled high with megapacks of toilet paper and SOS pads and animal crackers. Broekel had more boxes here, lined up on a high shelf. Again, I recognized very few of the names—Snirkles, French Pastry, Old Nick, Best Pals, Honest Square, Forever Yours. (As a matter of fact, Forever Yours was the dark chocolate version of the Milky Way, which had been introduced in the thirties then abandoned. It has since been reintroduced, as the Milky Way Midnight.) On the table below this display, next to a paper cutter, Broekel had a stack of old advertisements mounted on poster board.

"Where'd you get all these?" I said.

Broekel picked up the ad on top. "This one came from the *Delineator*. That's a magazine. It's from 1926."

"How did you find it?"

"I found people with old wrappers and old ads and I just bought them."

I grow puppyish when afforded the chance to discuss candy, but Broekel exuded the grim intensity of an archivist. His chief priority was to make sure everything got seen. Out of the pantry we went, down the hall, to a bank of shelves packed to overflowing with candy tchotchkes: fridge magnets, key rings, toys, PEZ dispensers, piggy banks. This was not what Broekel wanted to show me.

What he wanted to show me was a pair of shoulder-high green file cabinets tucked behind the shelves. He opened the one on the left. It was full of candy wrappers, alphabetized by company and filed in folders—hundreds, thousands of wrappers wedged together in crinkled sediments. Broekel didn't know exactly how many he had, but he figured around 20,000. He opened the file cabinet on the right. "These are the foreign ones." He opened the second drawer down. "More foreign ones."

Before I could ask Broekel how, exactly, one acquires 20,000 candy wrappers, he was off to another room, a kind of workshop area. The ceiling was decorated with old movie posters. A wooden plaque over the door read, I FINALLY GOT IT ALL TOGETHER, BUT I FORGOT WHERE I PUT IT. On the opposite wall was an honorary degree from Illinois College awarded to Rainer Luthar Broekel (it took me a moment to make the connection) and beneath this a colorful poster with a rooster exhorting the world to buy the Chicken Dinner candy bar. Broekel pointed to a large, black carrying case. It looked like the kind of thing Atticus Finch might have lugged around.

"Candy box," Broekel said.

With some difficulty, he wrestled the box off the sill and onto the floor. He unsnapped the latches and folded back the top to reveal two trays of candy, one with a dozen packs of LifeSavers and the other with a Sky Bar, some licorice, and a few pieces too warped to identify. I was not much impressed. Then Broekel knelt down and pulled these trays apart, and a third and fourth tray appeared, then a fifth and a sixth. He kept pulling until fourteen trays of candy were accordioned out before us in neat tiers, an entire portable candy rack stretching four feet across and including 30 different candy bars, gum balls, caramels, hard candies, Kits, Sen-sen, something called Lik-M-Aid, and something else called Coco-Melo.

"This is from the 1950s," he said. "It was used by a salesman in western Pennsylvania. He would carry this around to show what he had to offer and the merchant would place his order. It cost me $550. This is all the original stuff that was in there. The Snickers and Milky Way, those are from the 1930s." Broekel stared down at his pièce de résistance and flashed his bottom row of teeth in a shy smile. "That pretty much does it."

THE LOVE SONG OF RAY LUTHAR BROEKEL

Broekel seemed to feel that our visit had drawn to a close. I explained that I had a few more questions and we returned to the den and settled down across from one another. On the table next to me sat a tiny vending machine from the 1930s, which had been used to sell one-cent Hershey bars.

I asked Broekel if he'd always been interested in candy.

"Not really," he said.

"How did you decide to start writing about candy bars?"

"Well, I'm a writer." He pointed to a shelf across the room. "All those books up there, those are mine. I've written more than 200. Most of them are informational in nature." Broekel's speech had a nasal, humming quality, as if perhaps he were speaking through a tube that was underwater.

It was not entirely clear to me that he could hear my questions. So I started talking louder: "BUT SOMETHING MUST HAVE INSPIRED YOU TO WRITE ABOUT CANDY BARS, SIR."

Broekel paused. "Nothing had been written about them. People had written about candy, but not candy bars. The idea just came to me and I went downtown and got a couple of candy bars and looked at the wrappers and called the manufacturers to get more information. At a certain point, I looked around and realized I had a book on my hands."

"Right," I said. "Okay." I leaned back in my chair, waiting, in vain, for Broekel to elaborate. "What was the response?"

"I did a book tour sponsored by the National Confectioners Association. But the book went out of print while I was on tour."

"Why did you think the book didn't sell?"

"People didn't buy it."

"How did you decide to write the second book?"

"I got more information."

"Would you call yourself the foremost candy bar historian in the world?"

"Yes."

"Are there any others?"

"Not that I know of."

"Do you have a sweet tooth?"

"Not particularly."

Broekel looked at me with his watery blue eyes. It occurred to me, as I sat there trying to think of what to ask him next, that much of the reason I'd stopped reporting was because of situations like this. They required a certain tolerance for artifice; both parties had to stick to the script—the intrepid reporter, the eager subject—and even if they played their parts to the hilt, the result was a performance, an imitation of life. If one or both parties failed (and we were both failing here) the result was excruciating silence.

I glanced around the den. One entire wall was covered with lapel buttons. BURN POT, NOT PEOPLE. I'M A JAZZ BABY. BUNKER IN '72. BAN DDT. It was obvious that Broekel was a purebred collector, that any effort to explore his personal psychology was doomed. Stick to the collectibles, I told myself.

"What's your favorite piece?" I asked him.

"Dream Bar," Broekel said.

He got up and gingerly removed a box from the shelf. The front cover was a full-color lithograph of a boat, a schooner of some kind, covered with children. The children were all dressed in nightgowns and pajamas. The deck was covered with pillows and blankets. The rails were actually bedposts. Above them, a yellow crescent hung against the night sky and the stars twinkled madly. The sea was an inky blue-and-black sheen. The effect of the image was hypnotic. It captured the soft, fluid logic of the dream world, a place where children could peacefully sleep while waves licked at their toes. Broekel brought me a second box of the same vintage, this one for Milky Way—a surreal landscape, with billowing palm trees and a green-and-orange cloud system. There was no need to ask him why he favored these pieces. They were the sort of illustrations that belonged in a museum. One could imagine a young artist, an Andrew Wyeth or Maurice Sendak say, sitting in some tiny office during the Depression, creating these wild visions. They made the other boxes, the more modern stuff, look like, well, packaging.

Broekel sat down in his chair again. I sensed another wretched silence coming on. Thankfully, there was a knock on the door and Broekel went to answer it. He reappeared with a FedEx package. Inside was a Mounds wrapper from 1945, which he had lent to PBS for a documentary they were preparing about a radio correspondent who had been sponsored by Mounds.

I asked Broekel to tell me about the most interesting candy bar he'd come across.

"What do you mean, 'interesting'?" he said.

"Well, like, the one with the most interesting ingredients."

Broekel thought about this. "Vegetable Sandwich," he said finally.

"What's that?"

"I've got a picture," he said.

He walked out of the room and returned with a magazine article he'd written on ten candy bar classics. Number two was the Vegetable Sandwich, a bar introduced during the health craze of the 1920s. The wrapper showed a bright medley of veggies—celery, peas, carrots, cabbage. The legend read:

A DELICIOUS CANDY MADE WITH VEGETABLES. Dehydrated vegetables, to be exact, covered in chocolate. There is no need to elaborate on the wrongness of this product, though I feel duty bound to report that one of the manufacturer's taglines was WILL NOT CONSTIPATE. Yum. Amazingly, disturbingly, Vegetable Sandwich was not the only entry in the dehydrated vegetable candy bar derby. There was also the Perfect Bar (WE HAVE COMBINED IN THIS CONFECTION DEHYDRATED VEGETABLES RICH IN VITAMINS AND BRAN!).

Broekel's shelf also boasted a vintage 3 Musketeers box. I have never had much respect for the modern bar. I will certainly eat them, but I tend to lose interest rather quickly and often resort to coaxing the filling out with my fingers, so that I'm left with a delicate chocolate shell. The name, also, has always perplexed me. In what way does this mono-filling candy bar, this dull brick of nougat, express threeness, let alone Musketeeritude? I had heard the well-trafficked rumor that 3 Musketeers was originally the name given to the Milky Way and that, through some royal industrial mix-up, the names had gotten reversed. But this struck me as a typical candy canard, wishful and harebrained. Broekel's box solved this mystery. There, flanking a vivid portrait of the three soldiers with swords aloft, were the words CHOCOLATE, VANILLA, AND STRAWBERRY, 3 BARS IN A PACKAGE FOR FIVE CENTS.

I asked Broekel if he remembered the three-bar era.

"I was at the factory when the first bars came off the assembly line."

"Wow," I said. "When would that have been?"

"Some time in the thirties."

I waited (again) for Broekel to elaborate. He did not. We had reached another one of those conversational cul-de-sacs. Broekel sighed. I sighed. The room sighed. I asked Broekel if he would sign my copy of *The Great American Candy Bar Book*. He picked up a pen from an end table and scrawled his name.

Upstairs, Broekel's wife, Peg, was talking on the phone.

"What does your wife think of all this?" I asked him.

"It's a hobby of mine."

"I guess it could be worse," I said. "You could be a beer can collector."

"I collected those for a while," Broekel said.

I remembered that in his book, Broekel had mentioned the idea of converting his archive into a candy museum. I asked him if that plan was still alive.

He shook his head again.

"What do you plan to do with all this stuff?"

"I really don't know," he said.

It was a solemn moment. I could foresee a day, in the not-too-distant future, in which his remarkable trove would be boxed up and put in storage. Or worse yet, thrown away. I felt like telling him I'd be happy to serve as the executor of that portion of his estate focused on candy bars. But this was wildly presumptuous, given that he seemed not to like me very much. So I settled for asking to borrow a copy of his second book, *The Chocolate Chronicles,* before I took my leave. It was an oversized paperback, the spine badly tattered, the pages coming loose.

WELCOME TO THE BOOM

It is probably overstating the case to suppose that Broekel's interest in candy bars stems from a need to reconnect to his childhood. But his history—which I did eventually wrestle out of him—bears mentioning. His family came to the United States from Germany in 1927 and settled in Evanston, outside Chicago. He was four years old. America was in the thrall of its first and most intense candy bar boom, fueled by the return of the doughboys. Nickel bars were ubiquitous. Every confectioner in the country produced at least one; the big companies produced dozens. The variety would have been especially dizzying in the Chicago area, which was rapidly overtaking Boston as the nation's candy capital. This was an era before the onslaught of the modern snack industry, with its avalanche of chips and cookies. Aside from Hershey's, there was no such thing as a national brand.

It is virtually impossible for a consumer today to understand the candy bar landscape that a young Ray Broekel would have encountered. In fact, Broekel told me that there have been more than 100,000 brands of candy bars introduced in this country, nearly a third of them in the years between World War I and the Great Depression. Even if he is off by a factor of two (and I tend to doubt he is) the numbers are boggling.

This is what makes Broekel's books—both of which are out of print—such compelling reading. It is certainly not the prose, which tends toward skittish wordplay. Here, for instance, is the way Broekel introduces a section on the candy maker Peter Paul in *The Great American Candy Bar Book:* "Carmen Miranda was a singer known as The Brazilian Bombshell. Wearing elaborate dresses and huge headdresses laden with fruit, she appeared in numerous movies in the 1940s and early 1950s. What did Carmen Miranda have to do with a candy bar? Nothing. But something else from Brazil did: the Brazil nut." Right.

Broekel's obsession with pure documentation blossomed as he delved further into his research. By the time he wrote *The Chocolate Chronicles,* in 1985, he had dropped most of the rhetorical flourishes. This second volume reads like a dutiful compendium of facts. Given the commercial failure of the first book, it seems odd that he would attempt a second book at all. But this is missing the point. Broekel no longer viewed himself as an author in the traditional sense—that is, someone hoping to find an audience for his work—but as a collector of information. His obligation was chiefly to history.

Reading over *Chronicles,* one is struck by the strange, incantatory poetry of the brand names: Love Nest, Smile-a-While, Alabama Hot Cakes, Old King Tut, Gold Brick, Prairie Schooner, Subway Sadie, Oh Mabel!, Choice Bits, Long Distance, Big Alarm, That's Mine, Smooth Sailin, Red Top, It's Spiffy, Daylight, Moonlight, Top Star, Heavenly Hash, Cherry Hits, Cheer Leader, Hollywood Stars, Strawberry Shortcake, Ping, Tingle, Polar Bar, North Pole, Sno King, Mallow Puff, B'Gosh, Dixie, Whiz, Snooze, Big Chief, Firechief, Wampum, Jolly Jack, Candy Dogs, Graham Lunch, Tween Meals, Hippo Bar, Old Hickory, Rough Rider, Bonanza!

I am but skimming the surface, here. Broekel notes, for instance, that the Sperry Candy Company of Milwaukee, by no means a huge operation, turned out the following bars between 1925 and 1965: Chicken Dinner, Fat Emma, Straight Eight, Pair o Kings, White Swan, Prom Queen, Cold Turkey, Chicken Spanish, Denver Sandwich, Cool Breeze, Club Sandwich, Coco-Mallow, Coco Fudge, Big Shot, Cherry Delight, Hot Fudge–Nut, Almond Freeze, Mint Glow, Koko Krunch, and Ripple.

Nor did Broekel stop after the second book. Instead, he launched a homemade quarterly called the *Candy Bar Gazebo,* consisting almost entirely of Xeroxed candy wrappers gathered by him and a small stable of fellow candyfreaks (in the Broekelian nomenclature: "Foreign Correspondents" and "Roving Ambassadors"). In print, as in life, Broekel remained largely unburdened by the rigors of analysis. Broekel put the magazine out for nearly a decade and he still had most of the back issues, organized by quarter, in his basement. The editor's note atop his final edition, published in winter 1995, provided a flavor of the endeavor: "All good times must come to an end, and that's why this will be the last issue of *Candy Bar Gazebo*. News about old candy bars and old candy companies has been getting more and more difficult to obtain, and columnist Harry Levine of England passed away August 11, 1995."

It should be clear that Broekel had gone completely and wonderfully bonkers by this time. I found his work irresistable. For the greenhorn candyfreak, it was like stumbling upon a hidden trove of unprocessed data. What was most fascinating about this data was not the origin or content of the bars themselves—the usual suspects all accounted for—but the way in which manufacturers sought to distinguish their brands.

The most common ploy was to link a bar to a figure from popular culture: Charles Lindbergh begat both the Lindy and Winning Lindy. Clara Bow begat the It bar. Dick Tracy had his own bar. So did Amos N Andy and Little Orphan Annie and

Betsy Ross and Red Grange. Babe Ruth had a fleet of them, though the Baby Ruth, as any aficionado will tell you, was named after President Grover Cleveland's daughter. Bars such as Zep and Air Mail were introduced to capitalize on the new allure of aviation. The Pierce Arrow was one of several bars named after a luxury car. The Big Hearted Al was named after failed presidential candidate Al Smith. Other bars celebrated popular expressions (Boo Lah, Dipsy Doodle), exotic locales (Cocoanut Grove, Nob Hill, 5th Avenue), dance crazes (Tangos, Charleston Chew), local delicacies (Baby Lobster), and popular drinks (Milk Shake, Coffee Dan).

Other brands invoked the glamour of hit songs (Red Sails), carnival attractions (Sky Ride), quiz shows (Dr. IQ), high culture (Opera), even poets (Longfellow). The Longfellow is not to be confused with its inflammatory-sounding contemporary, the Long Boy Kraut. This moniker, contrary to my initial wishes, was not coined to exploit anti-German sentiment but because the bar's coconut resembled pickled cabbage.

One did not have to be nationally famous to merit a candy bar. Several New England brands were named after the evangelical preacher George S. Needham. The Yale candy company named the Blue Boy bar after local football star Albie Booth. A Minneapolis firm paid tribute to a local tribe with the Yacki-Hula bar, which pictured Native American maidens on the label. Candy bars pervaded every strata of culture. They were sold at burlesque halls and gambling dens and hawked by religious cultists such as John Alexander Dowie, whose followers raised money for their community by producing, among other bars, the Fig Pie.

One can see, in this frenzy of brands, the birth of modern marketing, the beginning of the link made between what we consume as entertainment and what we consume as sustenance. And make no mistake: candy bars were viewed, especially during the Depression, as sustenance. They were America's first fast food: cheap, self-contained, and (in the short-term at least) filling. For years, Broekel's favorite bar, the Chicken Dinner, carried a picture of a steaming chicken on the label, an effort to convey its wholesome attributes.

In fact, the candy bar boom that swept the nation after World War I provided an ideal laboratory for the marketing techniques that would soon dominate American commerce. Because candy bars were cheap, people bought lots of them every day. Because the ingredients were quite similar, there was no appreciably qualitative difference between one bar and the next. The most important thing was to get people eating your bar, to establish your taste as familiar and desired.

Names were one way to do this. But candy makers also resorted to publicity stunts. Most famously, in 1923 Otto Schnering, president of the Curtiss Candy Company, chartered a plane to drop thousands of Baby Ruths onto the city of

Pittsburgh. (There were no injuries reported.) Long before McDonald's and Burger King affixed game cards to their fries, candy companies were linking bars such as Put & Take and You Bet to the punchboard craze, a game of chance in which folks paid a few pennies to punch a prize board. No major aspect of the culture went unexploited. During Prohibition, the Marvel Company of Chicago made an 18th Amendment Bar, which boasted THE PRE-WAR FLAVOR and pictured a bottle of rum on the label. World War II spurred a battalion of militaristic bars: Flying Fortress, Jeep, Chevron, Buck Private, Big Yank, Commando.

What the best minds of the industry intuited was that establishing a solid brand name was the only way to survive over the long haul. This required aggressive advertising, a national distribution system, a fierce sales force, and the means to produce huge numbers of bars. While their competitors floundered about, guys like Milton Hershey and Forrest Mars were automating their factories, buying out competitors, and stockpiling raw ingredients. As a result, the industry sped ahead on a kind of hyperglycemic metabolism. Whereas the leaders of the auto companies, for instance, have consolidated only in the past decade or so, the candy giants have been there, done that.

Toward the end of my visit, I told Broekel about my plan to visit a bunch of smaller candy companies so I could document these operations before they disappeared. I assumed Broekel would share my distress over the current state of the industry. But his logic was actually a lot subtler than mine. "My grandkids have more candy bars to choose from than I did," he pointed out. "When I was a kid, you see, I only knew about the candy bars available in my area."

This was the crowning irony of candy's golden age: very few people actually experienced it in real time. Unless you were a traveling salesman with a sweet tooth, you probably never tasted even a fraction of the candy bars produced in this country. And now that our country consists largely of upwardly mobile nomads, most of the exotic brands are gone anyway. What people want these days is a dependable oral experience, the comfort, as they hurl through airports and across state lines, of a few, familiar brands.

5

THERE ARE MEN UPON THIS EARTH WHO TREAD LIKE GODS

Shortly after the Broekel colloquy, a friend of mine brought me two candy bars that I had never seen before. They were called Five Star Bars and the reason I had never seen them before is because they are sold primarily at Bread & Circus, an upscale grocery chain (that is, one I do not frequent). The bars were slightly larger than snack size, but they had a queer and pleasing heft. Indeed, they weighed nearly as much as a full-size Snickers. I tend to steer away from gourmet candy—at least from the *purchase* of gourmet candy—but here they were, gifts, and didn't they look pretty? Yes, they looked so pretty in their embossed wrappers that I was actually a little frightened to open them.

My friend had no such compunction. She unwrapped the

Caramel Bar and took a bite. It was clear, simply from the way her mouth addressed the bar, that we were dealing with a different grade of freak. Her bite was smooth and concerted—there was an obvious density at play here—though interrupted by two muted snaps, both of which caused her a quarter-moment of anguish, followed by a twinge of delight, registered as a flushing upon her cheeks. She moaned. It was a lovely thing to hear.

This reaction was, in my view, restrained. I had never tasted anything like the Five Star. Fancy chocolates, truffles and so forth, are one thing. But this was a fancy candy *bar,* a complex and nuanced marriage of ingredients. There was caramel, obviously, but also roasted almonds and nuggets of dark chocolate. It was draped in a thin layer of milk chocolate. The interplay of tastes and textures was remarkable: the teeth broke through the milky chocolate shell, sailed through the mild caramel, only to encounter the smoky crunch of the almonds, and finally, the rich tumescence of the dark chocolate. You almost never see milk and dark chocolate commingled, but the effect in this bar was striking: The sweetness of the milk chocolate rushed across the tongue, played against the musky crunch of the nut, then faded. The bite finished with an intense burst of dark chocolate, softened by the buttery dissolution of caramel. What I mean here: there was a temporal aspect to the bar, a sense of evanescence and persistence. Because of the random placement of the almonds and dark chocolate, each bite offered a distinct combination. It was like eating several different bars at once.

The Hazelnut Bar was so: milk chocolate around a hazelnut paste (by which I really mean a rich hazelnut mousse) interspersed with crushed hazelnuts. If the bar had stopped here, well, as we Jews say: *Dianu*. It would have been enough. But there was something else going on with the bar, an ineluctable grittiness that conveyed a tang of vanilla.

"What is that?" I said. "It's like, what, a cookie?"

"More granular," my friend said. "Like tiny planes of sugar."

Yes, that was it. Planes. The geometric sort. Little vanilla-infused planes.

It will go without saying that I broke my long-standing boycott of gourmet groceries in order to seek out additional Five Star Bars. The ingredient list for the Five Star Peanut Bar was simple enough: peanuts, peanut butter, and crisped rice, enrobed in milk chocolate. But the taste was richer, more chocolaty, than expected. And for good reason: the peanut butter contained chunks of white chocolate. (The author is at a loss to explain how the otherwise loathsome white chocolate works in this confection, but it does.) The net effect was a bar at once crunchy and dense, a Whatchamacallit squared or, perhaps, cubed.

But it was the Hazelnut Bar that tweaked my heart. And

specifically, that mysterious texture. So I tracked down the manufacturer, Lake Champlain Chocolates, and called their headquarters in Burlington, Vermont, and spoke to their PR guy, Chris Middings. He knew exactly what I was talking about. ("That very fine crunchiness, yes, absolutely.") But he didn't know what accounted for it. He was elaborately apologetic for this, explaining that he'd just taken the job, and promised to e-mail me an answer.

A day later I received a brief note: "The ingredient in question is called feuilletine. It's actually a crushed pastry, frequently used in European candies." Feuilletine is best known to Americans in its uncrushed form, those thin, pie slice–shaped cookies that are placed in ice cream sundaes.

Chris also invited me to visit the factory any time I was in the area. "You can talk to Dave Bolton," he said. "Our chocolate engineer."

I suppose I was aware, in an abstract way, that there were men and women upon this earth who served in this capacity, as *chocolate engineers*. In the same way that I was aware that there are job titles out there such as bacon taster and sex surrogate, which is to say, job titles that made me want to weep over my own appointed lot in life. But I had never considered the prospect of visiting a chocolate engineer. I could think of nothing else for days.

I arrived at the factory at nine in the morning, alongside a bus full of seniors from Mount Kisco, New York. Chris appeared and led me to a small room tucked away in the back of the factory. This was Dave Bolton's lab. It looked very much like your basic junior high science lab, except that the counters were littered with bags of recent work product—chocolate-covered toffees and cocoa nibs—along with jugs of flavoring and a tiny panning machine that resembled a space helmet.

Dave himself was hunched over a counter, scrutinizing what looked like an overgrown Junior Mint. He looked up when we came in and, almost reflexively, held the piece out to me. The dark chocolate shell gave way to an intense burst of sweet, chewy fruit. The texture was soft enough to yield to the teeth, yet firm enough to absorb the musky undertones of the chocolate.

"What you're eating," Dave said, "is a dried cherry, infused with raspberry and covered in a Select Origin 75 percent dark chocolate." He held out the bag. "Have another."

Here is what I wanted to say to Dave Bolton at that precise moment: *Take me home and love me long time, GI.*

"This is what I do back here," he explained. "Sales comes to me and says: 'Dave: think cherries.' I research what's out there on the market already and what ingredients are available. The whole idea with this piece was to get away from canned cherries, but to retain an intense cherry flavor. Then, of course, I had to find a chocolate with high fruit overtones, because I wanted the marriage of a fruity chocolate to a piece of fruit."

Dave had a neatly trimmed beard and a beaked nose and powerful, low-hanging arms that swung as he trudged about his lab. He looked like a rabbi. Or a navy cook. I couldn't decide. "People tend to think of chocolate in simplistic terms," he said. "But there's a tremendous variation based on where it's grown." He turned and grabbed a few boxes from the shelf behind him. These were his Select Origin chocolates, each from a different part of the world. They came in disks about the size of dimes. Dave's favorite, at the moment, was Tanzania. He was also a big fan of Cuba. "My first question, when I come up with a new piece, is always: What sort of chocolate makes the most sense?" He reached for the Santo Domingo and popped a few pieces into his mouth. "This has such an intense, smoky flavor. It would be best for a pastry. And it would be wonderful with figs or a fruit like that. A brown fruit."

It was now clear I was in the presence of freak genius. But Dave's approach to chocolate was actually pretty low-key, in the context of the new foodie movement which has sprung up around fine chocolate. This movement has, alas, spawned its own insufferable rhetoric, such that, in reading over various high-end chocolate catalogs, you are likely to encounter descriptions of this ilk: *A saucy single-bean, grown exclusively in the shady lowlands of Ghana and harvested on alternating*

Tuesdays, at dusk. Notes of cardamom and oak predominate, with an insouciant creosote finish. (Those familiar with other luxury foods—wine and coffee, for instance—are no doubt familiar with this process: the curdling of expertise into hauteur.) The new chocolate specialty products are equally pretentious. I ask you, does the world truly need a bar infused with hot masala? The latest rage, as of this writing, is super-concentrated chocolate, with a cocoa content in the 90 percent range, a trend that will, in due time, allow us to eat Baker's Chocolate at ten bucks a square.

In some sense, though, this decadence is a return to the pre-Columbian days of cocoa, when the bean was viewed as a gift from the god Quetzalcoatl and considered the domain of royalty. Five hundred years later, *Theobroma cacao* (literally: food of the gods) remains the single most complex natural flavor in the world. Flavorists have been trying to reproduce the taste for decades—and they're nowhere near doing so. This is because chocolate is made up of more than 1,200 chemical components, many of which give off distinct notes, of honey or roses or even spoiled fish. There's even one chemical in chocolate that's cyanide-based. This is to say nothing of chocolate's oft-touted psychoactive ingredients, which include caffeine, theobromine (increases alertness), phenylalanine and phenylethylamine (both known to induce happiness), and anandamide, which is similar to THC (yes, stoners, *that* THC).

In truth, most of the brouhaha over these chemicals is trumped up. They only occur in trace amounts. The main reason chocolate is the ultimate physiological freak is because it's half sugar and half fat.

FEUILLETINE, REVEALED

Dave came to Lake Champlain fifteen years ago. At the time, he signed on as a part-time truffle maker to help out his friend, owner Jim Lampman, during the Christmas rush. But he fell in love with the manufacturing process. As the business grew, he agreed to become chief of new product development. This, of course, included the Five Star Bars, which have become the company's signature product line.

"Those are all recipes we created," Dave said. "The Caramel Bar took us two years to figure out how to produce. Now, the Fruit and Nut Bar came much faster. I know it sounds silly, but I literally dreamed that candy bar. I dreamed of putting those precise ingredients together and came into the lab and made the bar in one or two tries. I'd read about Janduja chocolate, which is a very soft chocolate, the 'chocolate of love' according to the Italians. I figured it would go well with dried fruit and nuts."

When I told Dave that I'd never tried the Fruit and Nut Bar, he looked stricken and sent Chris to fetch one. With a delicacy any mohel would envy, he sliced the bar into thin slabs. The chocolate had a creaminess I associated with ganache, against which rose the chewier textures of raisins and pecans.

"The bar has a great finish," Dave noted, "because the nuts and fruit last a little longer than the chocolate. They clean the palate."

"What about the Hazelnut Bar?" I said.

Hazelnut, it turned out, had been especially tricky to devise. Dave spent months attempting to find the perfect ratio of feuilletine to chocolate. This was simple enough for a small batch. But somehow, moving to a large batch, there'd be too much chocolate, not enough crunch, or the other way around, and he'd have to start from scratch again. By the end, he was up to 50 percent feuilletine by volume, about 15 to 18 percent by weight. "This process is literally what we've built the company on," Dave said, "finding the proper proportion of flavors and textures."

He, too, had a healthy fascination with feuilletine. The Europeans, he informed me, call it a cereal, though it's really just the scrap from a patisserie cookie. It had become so popular as an ingredient that it was now mass produced. I imagined a whole army of men in puffy white hats and sterilized sneakers stomping on a sea of helpless patisseries and yelling curses in French, a sort of anger management thing for pastry chefs. Dave pulled a box from the shelf and pulled back the flap. I was alarmed to discover that feuilletine looked a lot like fish food. (In the interests of fairness, I should mention that Lindt makes a spectacular dark chocolate bar filled with feuilletine and hazelnut cream, which, thank God, is virtually impossible to find in this country, and which I know about only because my father/enabler recently sent me a bar from Switzerland.)

"Let me tell you a story," Dave said. "I was on a plane flying back from Baltimore and the guy next to me pulled out a Five Star Peanut Bar and put it down on the tray table thing and cut it in half and said: 'Would you like to try the best piece of candy you've ever eaten?' I just looked at the guy and said: 'I *invented* that bar.' "

This was the glory of his job. But Dave assured me there was a fair bit of grunt work, as well. A good example: the raspberry truffle debacle. A few years ago, he used a raspberry filling that consisted of canned raspberries cooked in vodka and strained through cheesecloth. Then Lake Champlain decided to get certified as kosher and the rabbi wouldn't accept that process because of the alcohol. Dave had to invent a filling similar enough that the public wouldn't know he'd modified the recipe. This took well over a year of trial and error. Lampman would walk by his lab and snarl, "Where's that raspberry truffle?" He finally came up with a combination of all-natural raspberry concentrate and raspberry jam.

The rabbis weren't the only ones Dave had to please. Lake

Champlain also had a group of tasters who gathered twice a year to sample new products. Dave had created a whole series of creams recently. Only one made it to market. "It can be pretty unnerving," he said. "I'll present a piece I think is marvelous and they'll say, 'This is crap!' I had a lemon-ginger cream I was pretty excited about, but they said it was too over-the-top. I have to keep my ego out of it."

Naturally, I asked Dave what cream got approved.

Mango, he told me. He suggested we go try one. This meant heading out to the production floor, which was just fine with me. Every candy bar factory smells like chocolate. But the scent at Lake Champlain was intoxicating. This was because they used a chocolate made for them by a Belgian company, one that I would grade as—to use the technical term—*totally ass-kicking*. The factory was impeccably clean. It was not only the cleanest factory I'd ever visited, it may have been the cleanest *room* I'd ever visited. A few of the twisting, overhead pipes had been painted in bright primary colors, which lent the operation a Yellow Submarineish feel.

We arrived just as the chilled hazelnut bars were being popped from their molds and lined up on a conveyor belt to be run through the enrober. A few feet away, a machine shaped like a pommel horse was spinning a series of specially designed molds to create hollowed-out Santas. Nor were these your average Santas: they had detailed beards and white chocolate trim on their coats and hats, which had been painted into the molds. Round and round they spun, with slightly dazed expressions.

Dave hurried past the enrober to a sleek, new machine. It featured a set of pistons, which shot various liquid fillings into molds of chocolate with a sharp pop. They were still figuring out what products could be made with the machine. They could do inclusions, anything that wouldn't jam up in the pistons. But the viscosity had to be just right. Lake Champlain had gotten big enough, as a company, that Dave now had to worry about whether they could mass-produce a piece. "Years ago," he said, "all I had to do was figure out the flavor. Now we're into flavor and technology." Dave gazed at the machine, a little morosely. The machine hissed and popped.

"Mango cream," I said.

"Right," said Dave.

We spent the next few minutes trying to locate a mango cream. Dave kept opening all these hidden doors. There were scraps of chocolate everywhere, little mutant truffles and Five Star Bars that had failed to pass muster, which I wanted very badly to snatch and stick in one of my pockets, as I feared otherwise they would be thrown away. Chris assured me he was having a selection of seconds put together for me.

The mango cream proved to be a milk chocolate piece, slightly larger than a gum ball, filled with a sweet, yellowish cream. "I would have liked a thicker center," Dave muttered. "But there were viscosity issues."

He made his way over to a large plastic bucket, which was filled with a moist white substance. "Smell," he said.

The aroma of coconut was overpowering. It was like I'd stuck my head inside a giant Thai food sauna.

"You know we'd like to have a fifth Five Star Bar," he said. "So I've been playing around with the idea of a Coconut Bar."

I told Dave, as politely as I could, that I thought this was a *very* bad idea, not least of all because of the creepy dead-skin texture of shredded coconut.

He nodded. "Try a little bit of this."

To my shock, the substance had all the tropical wallop of coconut but a mouthfeel that was smooth and buttery.

Dave had found a company to manufacture this ingredient for him, all natural and kosher for Passover. He was well into considering the elements that might make up the rest of the bar: chocolate chips, dried fruit, possibly the cherries he'd been working with, and a dark chocolate, to balance the sweetness of the coconut. He was not about to introduce a fifth Five Star Bar unless it stood up to the other four. He was adamant about this point and I did not, for a moment, doubt him.

We headed back to the quiet of the lab. Dave plainly felt most comfortable here, amid his various ingredients, where he was free to improvise, to mix and melt and create. He had me sample some of his recent creations, including a dark chocolate–covered almond which tasted (curiously enough) a lot like the chocolate-covered graham crackers I had worshipped as a kid.

I confessed that I'd sort of hoped the fifth Five Star Bar would showcase coffee. Dave told me that he'd been working on a bar infused with coffee. He'd already tried sixteen or seventeen different extracts, none of which passed muster. Not long ago, Lampman had come to him with what he described as the perfect coffee flavor. He and Dave then set about trying to figure out how this extract had been made. Lampman felt certain that cocoa butter was somehow involved. "So what we did," Dave said, "was we got some good French roast and brewed it in cocoa butter and let it steep and strained it out and there it was. The exact same product. A lot of my knowledge has come that way: eating something and then trying to figure out what it is I'm eating."

"Do you ever get sick of chocolate?" I asked.

"Sure," Dave said. "Sometimes after I leave here I've got to go eat a head of cauliflower. Then again, I get to eat some of the best chocolate in the world. And I'm a chocolate snob, personally. I can't even eat a Hershey's bar. It's got maybe 22 percent chocolate liqueur, and that sour milk flavor. I mean, it's like baby vomit to me." It turned out that Dave had been born in England. His parents had immigrated to America, but much of his family had stayed in England, and he'd grown up eating European chocolate.

I had now taken two hours of Dave's time, and it was clear he had work to do. The idea of leaving his lab, however, made me a little panicky. I wanted to stay. I wanted, in some sense, never to leave. It occurred to me that Dave might need an apprentice. He indicated that he was not really in the market for an apprentice. He did promise to put in a good word for me when it came time to select a new member for the tasting panel.

This was certainly a kind gesture. But what I really wanted was this: for Lake Champlain—with its exquisite attention to intricacies of flavor and texture—to open a can of whoopass on the mainstream candy market. I asked Dave, as a kind of desperate parting shot, if this could ever happen. He shook his head. The company was toying with the idea of introducing a product in the impulse buy market, like the Ferrero Rocher, a German gourmet candy that had managed to fight its way onto the grocery racks. But that was as far as they could go.

So I headed out of the lab feeling a bit deflated. Most Americans, I knew, would never taste the glories of the Five Star Bar. They would continue to chomp through their PayDays and Fast Breaks, unaware of these deeper pleasures. A second tour group of seniors, this one from Maine, was milling about the retail store at the front of the factory, fretting over prices. This was certainly a bummer. But then, before I could launch into one of my self-thwarting diatribes, Chris the PR guy appeared and handed me a large bag of seconds—which included a raft of mango creams—and I felt much better.

FREAK FETISH

My spirits remained high, even after I'd plowed through the freebies. Dave Bolton had invigorated me, precisely because he was willing to talk about the experience of the world in his mouth, and with great precision. In the weeks following my visit, I found myself asking (alright, grilling) my friends more explicitly about their various freak fetishes.

Carmen told me she was fond of placing her favorite candy bar, Snickers, under her thigh, so as to warm the bar to a state where it was just on the verge of melting. My own Snickers methodology, by contrast, was to freeze the bar and cut it into thin sections. I did so not just because I'm a cheapskate (though I certainly am a cheapskate) but because I enjoyed seeing a cross section of each bite, and because I like caramel best when it's chilled to a taffyish consistency.

Evan revealed, with little prompting, his childhood method for eating Whoppers, which was to bore a tiny hole in the chocolate coating, then to use his saliva to dissolve the malted milk interior, leaving a perfectly intact milk chocolate ball. He would then place the Whopper back in the family candy bowl, and watch, with the unbridled sadistic pleasure of a nine year old, as some unlucky adult chomped down on the hollowed-out ball. "Or you can also just eat them yourself," he told me. "They taste especially good if you enjoy the taste of chocolate and your own spit."

At the risk of further offending the squeamish, I must report that an old college pal told me, in a moment of tipsy overconfession, that he had recently used a Butterfinger to liven up the proceedings with his girlfriend. (This did not disgust me in the least, as my idea of high-concept pornography often involves naked women and candy bars.) Several friends described an allegiance to Wint-O-Green LifeSavers, based on the fact that they spark when bitten in the dark. Another told me she buys the York Peppermint Pattie mostly because the bar produces an audible sigh when broken in half.

In other words, people don't just have favorite candy bars, but particular oral strategies for eating them. M&M's are the best example; they represent a kind of confectionery Rorschach. Putting aside the basic question of peanut versus plain, you might consider this: Do you eat single or multiple? Do you bite or suck? If you suck, do you store the M&M's on your tongue, or between cheek and gum? Do you allow the outer shell to melt completely, or do you smoosh the piece once the candy coating has become delicate enough? I myself enjoy balancing each piece between my front teeth and biting down on the circumference, thus popping off one half of the candy shell. I then work off the second half with my tongue, leaving (if all goes well) a pod of pure chocolate, which I soften on the roof of my mouth.

What does this say about me, this bite-and-suck approach? Should it be an issue in my therapy? And does it matter that I still smell my food before I put it in my mouth? Or that I have been known to take a bite of a cookie at my weekly poker game and, if the flavor or texture fails to please, place the rest of it back on the plate? What to make of the fact that I still bite Clark Bars lengthwise, as Manny De Costa taught me? Or that, at the urging of my brother Dave, I ate several M&M's out of the gutter at age four?

This will not be on the final.

6

THE OFFICIAL DARK HORSE FREAK OF PHILADELPHIA

I was bombing down State Road in north Philly with my pal Jena, pretty much totally lost, when my cell phone rang. It was Carl Goldenberg, the president of Goldenberg Candy.

"Where are you?" he said. "Have you passed the prison yet?"

"The prison?" I said.

"We're across the street from the prison," Carl said. "The prison is pink."

I turned to Jena, who was driving. "Have we passed a pink prison?"

"I don't think so," she said.

I told Carl I thought we were close by, as I wanted him to believe in my essential competence, which was questionable at best, and perhaps less than questionable in matters of navigation.

"Maybe we should turn around," Jena said.

We turned around.

State Road was not the most attractive part of Philly. It seemed to consist of two basic business elements: warehouses and shops offering various auto repair options. After a few blocks, Jena pointed out her window. "Isn't that accordion wire?" she said. Why, yes it was. And weren't those guard towers? And there in the distance, that vast, bunkerlike, pink building . . . "How did we miss *that*?" Jena said.

We pulled into the parking lot across the street from the prison, still not quite sure if we were in the right place. Then Jena opened her door and the aroma of roasted peanuts hit us like a full-force gale and we were lifted up again, by roasted peanuts.

"This must be the place," she said.

I'd called the Goldenbergs a few weeks earlier, on the advice of a candy distributor in Cambridge. The Goldenbergs were one of the few true family operations left in the candy world, producers of a bar called Peanut Chews. I had never heard of it before, which Jena had some trouble believing.

"Peanut Chews," she said. "Come on. *Peanut Chews*."

My friend Laura in Baltimore adopted the same incredulous tone. "You know, Peanut Chews."

Well, I didn't know Peanut Chews. I'd never lived in Philly or Baltimore, the apparent Heartland of Peanut Chews.

"You found us," Carl said, ushering us into his office. "Good, good. Excuse the boxes."

I assumed, based on the boxes, that the Goldenbergs had just moved. Actually, Carl said, the move took place five years ago. It was taking him some time to settle in. He was delighted with the new factory, though. At the old plant, the female workers were often frightened when they had to walk to their cars at night. In this new location, the criminal element was, conveniently, locked up across the street. Carl smiled at Jena. He was an elegant, elderly gentleman, a bit of a flirt, with soft blue eyes and an avuncular manner. He led us out of his office and down a corridor that led to a white door.

"We have two different coatings and lots of different wrappers, but we only make one thing, really, and it all begins with the roasting of peanuts." With a flourish, he flung the door open.

I had not thought it possible that the scent of roasting peanuts could be any more intense than what we experienced in the parking lot. And I was wrong. The parking lot, after all, was an open-air venue, whereas the roasting room was an enclosed space. The dominant feature, not surprisingly, was the roaster itself, the main body of which looked like an overweight torpedo. One hundred and ten–pound sacks of peanuts, redskins trucked up from Georgia, were fed into this beast and spun around and around and blasted with fire.

A number of other things were done to these peanuts before they appeared again to the naked eye. They were sucked up into an air conveyor, a process that helped cool them. They were relieved of their husks, which were blown down a quartet of long, square shafts running from the ceiling to just above the floor. (Each shaft emitted a lovely red mist of desiccated skins.) They were run through a metal detector and a split-nut blancher, which divided them in half. Finally, the nuts came pouring down a chute and onto a conveyor belt, where two workers in blue smocks plucked out any burned or disfigured specimens. These were some very busy peanuts.

"My father designed this whole system," Carl shouted, over the roar of the roaster. "He was a mechanical genius."

We spent a few minutes gazing at the huge, heated tanks used to store molasses and corn syrup, the two main liquid ingredients used in Peanut Chews. Carl showed us the room where the company stored its chocolate coating, in a chemical tank purchased from Eastman Kodak—presumably after a thorough cleaning—and outfitted with a steam jacket. Carl was careful to emphasize the word *coating* because Goldenberg uses what's known in the industry as compound—cocoa mass with soy lecithin providing the fat content instead of cocoa butter. They made the switch in the fifties, when both peanut and chocolate prices were skyrocketing. "The chocolate we were buying was awful anyway," he said. "We found the compound actually tasted a lot better with our center, which is crunchy and not as sweet."

A few yards from the peanut roaster, a fellow in chef's whites was pouring a white, gelatinous substance into a stainless steel kettle. "This is how our filling gets made," Carl said. He was reluctant to disclose the exact recipe, which had been handed down from his grandfather, other than to note that it included five different types of sugar, three of them liquid. He seemed more comfortable discussing what the filling wasn't: It had no milk and therefore wasn't a caramel. It wasn't a syrup. It wasn't a brittle. So what was it?

From what Jena and I could see, it was *goop*. (Yes, another technical term.) We watched as this golden-brown goop was piped from the kettle into another oddly torpedo-shaped tank, where the roasted peanuts were added. The blend, now lumpy with nuts, tumbled down a long chute, onto a wide white conveyor belt, where it was flattened by rollers into a slab about two feet across.

"In the old days, we used to have to pour each batch onto a marble slab and flatten it with paddles," Carl explained. "When it was cool enough, we cut it into large loaves and ran those through sizers, which crushed most of the peanuts. The system you're watching is called ConSlab, short for continuous slab, which means no one touches the candy until the consumer opens the wrapper. We were the first ones in the country to use ConSlab. The second one went to Charleston Chew."

The slab disappeared into a long cooling tunnel and emerged a hundred feet later. It was a gorgeous sight, this tongue of glistening golden goop with peanuts suspended inside. Regrettably, the knives came next. They cut the slab into two dozen half-inch strips, which were then gently pried apart.

I mentioned to Carl that the strips looked sort of like dreadlocks.

He looked at me blankly.

"Next," he said, "each of these strands gets cut into minis. There's a camera that measures to make sure we get the precise length. There's just one size. We package them differently. But the basic piece is what you're looking at." (Originally, Peanut Chews were made in full-size bars, but the company switched to bite-size pieces in the 1930s, at the request of movie house operators.) Carl gazed down with naked affection at the minis, chugging along in their uniform rows. He picked a bit of scrap off the side of the ConSlab. "Try this."

To be honest, I wasn't expecting much. What had I seen, after all? Peanuts. Goop. But the piece was absolutely exquisite, like a rich taffy, with a hint of molasses for body, and the peanuts provided a pleasing textural snap and a rush of smoked flavor.

Carl nodded. "Wonderful, isn't it? We'd love to be able sell it this way, straight off the line. We can't do that, obviously. But we do produce them to order, which means we ship them straight onto the shelves. They don't sit around in a warehouse."

With a sudden, courtly bow and hand wave, he presented a piece to Jena.

"It's so peanutty," Jena said.

"I never get sick of the taste," Carl said. "To me, nothing compares to a Peanut Chew. Snickers are terrible." His voice, in this cadenced tenor of disgust, called to mind Jackie Mason. "Compared to this—what? They drop a few peanuts in it and tell you there's peanuts. This is *all* peanuts. The filling is just there to keep the peanuts together."

Jena had never seen an enrober, so we stood there and listened to her make all the appropriate noises as the sheet of dark chocolate compound washed down onto the army of identical minis. When the time came, I laid a hand on her shoulder and coaxed her from her inaugural freaktrance and we moved on to the next cooling tunnel.

The finished pieces, now coated and gleaming, were put through a series of industrial calisthenics as they moved from rows of two dozen across to single file. This seems easy enough, but you tend not to realize how complicated a process becomes when it's mechanized. The minis were forced to make a little steeplechase leap onto a vibrating table and then hustled around a little circular track and sent whizzing toward the scary-looking wrapping machines, which were the source of considerable fascination to Carl, who spent many minutes detailing their function while I snuck Peanut Chew after Peanut Chew from the scrap table into my craw.

WEE WILLIE AND THE POP-A-LICKS RAGE

Carl led us back to his office. Jena asked him about how he stayed so thin working in a candy factory and Carl, now thoroughly smitten, noted that he'd just lost 20 pounds. The two of them discussed dieting for a while. Then they talked about downtown Philadelphia. Was a job offer in the offing? It was too early to tell.

Finally, I managed to get Carl to detail the history of the business. His grandfather, David Goldenberg, had come to Philadelphia from Romania in 1880. He was eighteen years old, the youngest of seven children. That was all Carl really knew about his origins because David, like most immigrants, had no interest in his own past. He found work at carnivals, selling cotton candy and caramel apples, eventually opening a retail store on Kensington Avenue. The entire family, his wife and seven children, lived over the store, where they all worked. They made cakes and ice creams, as well as sweets. The Goldenberg scion was, by all reports, a small man, but his appetite was legendary. He used to head down into the basement, where they did the baking, grab a fresh pie, plop a pint of ice cream on top, and eat the whole thing. This struck me as a totally excellent thing to do. It reminded me of my own favorite dessert growing up, aside from candy, which was a kind of goulash I prepared by crushing half a dozen Oreos into a bowl of Breyers mint chip ice cream, then placing my desk lamp directly over the bowl. (This was in the days before microwaves; I had to improvise.)

David eventually expanded his business to a double storefront and began selling candies to other businesses. World War I turned out to be his big break. The army needed ration bars. He took what had been a walnut loaf and used peanuts instead, because they were cheaper. When the war ended, the soldiers had a taste for the bars. Eventually the company began to ship Peanut Chews down the Delaware River to Baltimore. From there, wagon jobbers would distribute them as far as York.

By the thirties, demand had outstripped supply and Goldenberg relocated to a five-story plant. The company made everything back then: caramels, chews, lollipops. They had one whole floor devoted to fudge. Carl used to work in the fudge department during summers, mixing nuts in with a wooden paddle. The work added 50 yards to his tee shot. His favorite piece was a penny candy called Whip Its, a marshmallow rolled in toasted coconut. Goldenberg's most popular item, aside from Peanut Chews, was a hard caramel lollipop called the Pop-a-Lick. The sucker was popularized by a radio personality named Wee Willie, who hosted a program for kids. Indeed, his endorsement was so fervent that he sparked one of those kid-driven frenzies. For a while, the company couldn't make enough Pop-a-Licks to keep pace.

Goldenberg did brisk business during World War II because the company had quotas that allowed them to buy sugar and peanuts. It was strictly a seller's market then. But when the war ended everything changed. Suddenly, people could make fudge in their own kitchens. The candy market quickly glutted. Faced with slumping sales, David Goldenberg decided to liquidate the business in 1949.

That was fine with all the various relatives—except his youngest son, Harry, who wanted something to pass on to his sons. He made a crucial decision: to relaunch the company with just one product. While the old factory was shutting down, Harry designed a new plant. "I remember him drawing up those plans on our dining room table," Carl said. "He never graduated from high school, but he knew electricity. He was something of a genius when it came to machines. He could look at a broken wrapping device and diagnose the problem, like a good doctor can diagnose a physical problem."

Harry was also an astute businessman. He intuited, correctly, that there was enough demand for Peanut Chews to sustain a smaller, leaner operation. Goldenberg has maintained its core market, from Boston down the coast to Virginia, plus a few new markets, most notably in Florida.

"And then there's Korea," Carl said.

"Korea?" I said.

"Yeah, Korea." Carl shook his head in bemusement. "Our broker over there—this young man sells everybody. He competes with Mars and Hershey's. He was buying so much that I said to Ed, our guy in sales, 'What's going on?' I pictured a warehouse bulging at the seams. But it sells over there, as long as it's fresh."

I took this as a testament to the fact that tastes can be altered, in a market not already saturated with candy bars. But I wondered how, exactly, the company hoped to win new fans in America.

"Well, one thing we did," Carl explained, "we had one of those, I forget the term, where you gather people to discuss a particular thing . . ."

"A focus group?"

"Yeah, we did a focus group."

The focus group revealed that consumers viewed the Peanut Chews wrapper as old-fashioned. So the company updated the wrappers a few years ago. They also introduced a milk chocolate Chew. Aside from these measures, though, Goldenberg can't do much. They can't diversify. They can't advertise. And they can't pay slotting fees. (Winn-Dixie, the grocery chain, recently demanded $25,000 to stock Peanut Chews. Goldenberg had to demur.)

"Way back when, there were so many family businesses here in Pennsylvania," Carl said. "We even had an association. Every year, we'd have a convention in Redding. Each family took a different set of cottages. It was really so wonderful, all these aunts and uncles and cousins were there and you knew you were a part of something."

"What would happen if you tried to hold another one today?"

Carl laughed. "There wouldn't be anybody. The Blumenthals are gone. The Minters are gone. The Bachmans are gone. If my father hadn't done what he did, we'd be gone, too."

We had reached a place of melancholy. Carl gazed at Jena in a way that made the both of us want to rush forward and comfort him. But then he smiled, as if to say *Well, enough of that,* and he took us to the conference room to see a great variety of wrappers. We were soon joined by his son David, who, in marked contrast to his male forebears, was exceedingly tall and well muscled. He looked, with his thick glasses and sweet goofy smile, like a cross between Jerry Lewis and Lou Ferrigno.

David told us he'd wanted to become a vet when he was younger. "I wasn't raised to be a Chew," he said. "That's a little Chewish humor."

A brief silence ensued.

"Did your dad pressure you to join the family business?" I asked.

"Not really," David said. "I never hung out in the factory as a kid. But I used to come into the office to write papers in high school and whenever I smell those peanuts, if I haven't been in the factory for a while, it sends me right back to my youth. That smell has been with me for a long time."

"There was *great* joy when he called to tell me he was interested in the business," Carl interjected. "I never said anything to him, though. I knew better than that."

"He wrote me a letter," David said.

"That's right," Carl said. "I wrote him a letter."

David started with the company in 1977. He took over as plant manager six years later. In 1997, he became president. (I had the guy pegged as 35. He was 47.) The business he took over was much the same as the one his grandfather founded. It was the competition that had changed. The Big Three now controlled the racks. These were global companies with tremendous buying power. They were able to think long-term. The one factor they could not control was the consumer's desire for variety. "People don't just want two peanut products," David said, "Snickers and Baby Ruth."

The Big Three are well aware of that, though, which is why they keep introducing new peanut-based bars: Fast Break,

Snickers Cruncher, and so on. Another potential problem, as David acknowledged, was the shifting demographic. How was Goldenberg supposed to replenish the aging Peanut Chews fan base with younger devotees? For the moment, they were hoping new wrappers and special sale packs would help.

"We're never going to compete with the big guys," David said. "But we continue to do a good business. Sometimes I wish my great-grandfather could see what we've built here. I'd like to be able to bring him back, give me half an hour, and I could show him around. Then he could go back to wherever he was."

"Did you ever meet him?" I asked.

"No. But I got to work with my grandfather for twenty years. He was an absolute genius mechanically—"

"I told him," Carl said.

"Remarkable. He was a remarkable taster, too. He could taste something and tell you if it had vanilla or orange or whatever and I think I inherited that. My daughter got that from me."

David's kids, a boy and a girl, would be the fifth generation, if they decided to go into the family business. He had no plans to push them in this direction, though.

"I told him a long time ago, you can't plan to go into a family business," Carl said. "Because you just don't know if it's going to be around."

Several months after my visit, the family sold the business

to Just Born (best known as producers of Mike and Ike and the loathsome Marshmallow Peeps), ending 113 years of independent operation. Carl tried to be upbeat about the move. The plant would remain in operation, virtually all the workers still had jobs. But there was more than a hint of resignation in his voice. "You can't be a regional company in this environment anymore," he noted. "We just couldn't do it on our own."

On a brighter note: before we said good-bye, Carl gave us a box of 36 bars. Jena told me she wasn't such a huge fan of Peanut Chews, but I left most of them with her anyhow, figuring this is what Carl would have wanted. A few weeks later I received the following e-mail: "Peanut Chews gone. Am now addicted. Jena."

7

SOUTHERN-FRIED FREAK

I do know an unfortunate number of southerners, as a result of attending a university in North Carolina (state motto: Why Can't You Be More Polite?), and virtually all of them, when I mentioned candy bars, assumed that the Goo Goo Cluster would be at the top of my list. It was not. Part of the reason for this is that candy bars are not often grist for literary culture and thus have been spared the relentless invocation of other such southernisms as kudzu, moonshine, Co-Cola, and Shiloh.

Nonetheless, Goo Goos are by far the best-known candy bar in the South, and certainly the most ornate. They're giant turtle-looking critters, with marshmallow and caramel in the center and peanuts scattered on top. The Goo Goo Supreme, which features pecans rather than peanuts, was cited by no less an authority than Ray Broekel as his favorite candy bar in the world and he swore to me that I could find them up North, that he had, in fact, bought one just a couple of weeks earlier "in town." This led me on a wild-goose chase through the suburban precincts of Ipswich, where I would *not* recommend you look for a Goo Goo Cluster. Nor would I necessarily recommend that you fly down to Nashville, as I did, in order to track down a Goo Goo.

Then again, Goo Goo production is incredibly cool to watch, and Joanne, the marketing director for Standard Candy Company, is also incredibly cool (once you get to know her) and she will give you lots of free Goo Goos. The parenthetical caveat is the result of a lengthy series of phone calls and e-mails, during which I tried to determine on exactly which days Goo Goos would be in production, while Joanne tried to determine whether or not I was insane.

She was much nicer in person, an attractive, fortyish woman with a blond bob and the indefatigable enthusiasm of a camp counselor. On the day I showed up, a Monday, the Goo Goos were not in production. Joanne felt bad about this. She promised that if I came back the next day, I could watch Goo Goos being made, and, as a token of goodwill, she led me through the factory, which was busily cranking out a diet bar for a well-known weight-loss company. The diet bar consisted of: chocolate, crisped rice, and caramel.

I will leave it to the reader to determine just what sort of "diet" would encourage the consumption of these ingredients, though it bears mentioning that this product is but one in a tsunami of pseudo–candy bars, variously called PowerBars, Granola bars, Energy Bars, Clif Bars, Breakfast Bars, Snack Bars, Wellness Bars, and so on, all of which contain roughly the same sugar and fat as an actual candy bar—with perhaps a dash of protein sawdust thrown in—but only half the guilt, and stand as a monument both to shameless marketing and the American capacity for self-delusion, particularly in matters related to consumption (see also: frozen yogurt, fat-free chips, and low-calorie lard).

All this said, I enjoyed watching the production process, in particular the way the crisped rice rained down on the enrobed caramel bars—a hailstorm rendered in miniature. I was a little confused, though, as to why Standard was producing a diet bar for someone else.

Joanne explained, rather carefully, that Standard's core business was changing. They were doing a lot of contract manufacturing for other companies. She ticked off the names of four well-known brands, none of which I was allowed to cite by name.

Contract manufacturing is one of the best-kept secrets in the retail business. Here's how it works: Let's say you run a well-known upscale bakery chain. You want to expand into candy bars, but you don't have the means to make candy bars, and to acquire them would mean shelling out a lot of dough. What do you do? You find a company with production lines already set up and farm out the manufacturing grunt work to them.

However, you've got a brand name to uphold, consumers who expect that your products are made by your employees, in your factories, with the fine attention to detail that allows you to sell a corn muffin for two bucks and change. So you make sure that the company you contract with doesn't let it slip that they're the ones who make your product. The idea, in other words, is to save money *and* maintain brand prestige. The reason Joanne had such a hard time pinpointing when I should visit the plant, it turns out, is because Goo Goos are only in production ten days per month.

The next day Joanne led me to a conference room where she quickly outlined the history of the business. Standard began as a general line confectioner at the turn of the century, producing hard candies and chocolates. Then, in 1912, something remarkable happened: the owner and the plant manager got together in the kitchen and started playing around with various ingredients. The result was the first multi-ingredient candy bar ever produced. The precise origins of the name are not known, though it is generally thought to echo a baby's first utterance.

Goo Goos are most commonly recognized among country

music fans as a faithful sponsor of the *Grand Ole Opry,* a radio program I had not had the pleasure of hearing. "It's pretty cool," Joanne assured me. "At the end of the show, the stars say, 'God I love the Goo Goo!' and then the audience goes, 'They sure are good!' or something like that. I can't remember exactly what they say."

Joanne herself grew up in Michigan. Her parents moved to Georgia when she was in her twenties, and they got in the habit of bringing her Goo Goos when they visited. Her dad was a great fan, which meant, of course, that he was thrilled when Joanne got hired on at Standard, though he was now diabetic, which seemed a cruel irony.

Our first stop on the factory tour was a machine called the Continuous Cycle Starch Mogul, which was making the Goo Goo centers. It was as scary looking as the name suggests: a huge, clicking, clanking behemoth whose various pulleys, ramps, and chutes were coated in a white patina of cornstarch. The ground below looked as if Tony Montana had just thrown one of his special parties for one.

Joanne led me past the mogul and upstairs to a small, sweltering room where marshmallow and caramel were cooked up in stainless steel kettles. I watched a milky brown river of caramel flow through a hole in the floor, down into a hopper below and I thought: *caramel.* How perfect is caramel? What would happen if I stuck a finger into this caramel? Or a hand?

Just how much trouble would I be in here? I took a step toward the caramel and went into a nervous half-crouch just as Joanne, who had been bantering with one of the cooks, wheeled around.

"Are you okay?" she said. "You look funny."

The mogul worked like this: a stack of wooden trays was loaded into one side of the machine. Each of these was filled with cornstarch. A set of molds was pressed into the starch. In the case of Goo Goos, the molds were circular and about two inches across. These trays then trundled under the depositors, which squirted caramel and marshmallow into the molds. From there, they went to a cooling room to be cured overnight, allowing the cornstarch to absorb any excess moisture. This last step is the crucial feature of the mogul because it eliminates the stickiness that would otherwise make the production of most jellies and creams impossible. The mogul is used to make virtually all candies that begin as liquids. Switching from Goo Goos to, say, jelly beans is simply a matter of changing the molds.

Joanne and I arrived downstairs just as a stack of trays was being wheeled out from the curing room. These were loaded into the mogul, which flipped them over, sending the Goo Goo centers clattering onto a conveyor belt, while the cornstarch was sent whooshing over to a terrifying tented machine labeled SIFTER DISCHARGE, which shook violently in an effort to make sure the recycled cornstarch did not stick together.

The Goo Goo centers looked like, well, UFO ships circa 1954, if you can imagine such a ship composed of half caramel, half marshmallow, and dappled in cornstarch. They whizzed out from the mogul onto an escalating conveyor belt, which carried them into the adjacent room. Here, they were sent flying, willy-nilly, onto the enrobing line.

"Which goes on top," I said. "Caramel or marshmallow?"

"It doesn't matter," Joanne said.

"It doesn't matter?"

"Nope. Why would it matter?"

I was sort of at a loss. "Just because, you know, for consistency."

But the Goo Goo Cluster, as I was about to discover, was not some carefully calibrated candy bar with neat angles and computer-regulated ratios. It was a delightful mess. Even the production line was a mess. The initial enrober was draped in a clear tarp. A large, crinkled-steel vent of the sort I associated with the back of a dryer was angled through the tarp to blow the excess chocolate off the centers. The tarp was spattered with reddish-brown chocolate. The whole setup looked a little like open-heart surgery.

We moved down the line. The Goo Goo centers emerged from the enrober looking pretty uniform, ranked and shimmering in coats of wet chocolate. You would have never known that all hell was about to break loose, for we had reached . . . the *nut applicator*.

Yes, children, the nut applicator.

The nut applicator was a grooved circular device that sat just above the conveyor belt. A hopper fed roasted peanuts into the grooves of the nut applicator, which rotated slowly, dumping each grooveful of peanuts onto a particular row of Goo Goo centers. *Applying* the peanuts, I suppose I should say, except that *apply* is a little neat sounding, given the result. Some of the Goo Goos were enveloped in peanuts, double-stacked even, while others had large bare patches. Adding to the chaos was a huge vent which blasted air onto the Goo Goos from above, sending up squalls of red peanut skins.

"We do the first enrobing so the peanuts have something to stick to," explained Joanne, who had a commendable habit of nibbling on the roasted peanuts at the edge of the conveyor belt. The Goo Goos passed through a short cooling tunnel and over a little moat, into which the peanuts less successfully applied to the centers tumbled.

CHOCOLATE HAIKU

You will have to trust me when I tell you that I have seen a good number of enrobers at this point in my life. But I have never witnessed anything as sublime as the second enrober on the Goo Goo production line. Why? Because the curtain of chocolate that oozes down is so thick that the individual Goo Goos lose almost all sense of contour. They are drowned in chocolate, reduced to shiny amorphous lumps. And then, just as suddenly, reverse vacuums blow the chocolate off each piece and the force of the blower sends up tiny ripples and the Goo Goos reemerge, as in a time-lapse photograph, each inimitable lump and crag outlined.

"It's hard to explain to people how beautiful the process is," Joanne said. "The first time I saw this, it took my breath away."

I was almost entirely tranced out at this point and I remember mumbling something about the chocolate and the steel, the strangeness of their collaboration, some kind of haiku really:

Brown rivers released
From cold silver machines sing
for a stunned wet tongue

Joanne walked me to the end of the line, where the Goo Goos were emerging from the final cooling tunnel. She grabbed one for me and took one herself and we went to town. What do I want to say? The bar was more like an extremely gooey pastry. I bit through the thick outer crust of chocolate, hit a cluster of peanuts, then another layer of chocolate, before reaching the caramel/marshmallow patty. Because of this double enrobing process, chocolate was the dominant flavor. But the bar had a distinct undercurrent of coconut as well, the source of which is the chewy filling. I know this because Joanne later gave me a naked patty to eat. The Goo Goo was an absolute sugar bomb. Aside from the peanuts, the ingredients were all super sweet. The Goo Goo Supreme, topped with pecans rather than peanuts, was even sweeter, with a mellow maple aftertaste. So Joanne and I stood there wolfing down our Goo Goos. Because they were fresh off the line, the chocolate hadn't really had a chance to set, and this meant that they melted in our hot little hands. By the time we were through, we had chocolate on our fingers and at the corners of our mouths.

What struck me as most telling was the expression on Joanne's face, a nervous joy awakened in the soft flesh around her eyes. For people like Joanne and Manny and Dave Bolton—true freaks—this was the allure of working with candy: watching a fellow freak eat your goodies. This was why they were forever thrusting candy into my hands and beaming expectantly. Watching me eat wasn't just a vicarious affirmation of craftsmanship, but a celebration of the fundamental impulse toward pleasure. The world was a mean enough place, after all, especially if you worked at a struggling candy company.

Be that as it may, Joanne and I were now severely cranked on sugar, so we zinged along to the packaging area, covertly working at the bits of peanuts and caramel lodged in our teeth. Joanne had an unconscious compulsion to straighten the Goo Goos as they emerged from the wrapping machine. "An old habit from retail," she explained. "I did the same thing with clothes on the rack."

We watched a trio of Latin women packing the Goo Goos into boxes. They snatched two at a time off the conveyor belt, over and over, two at a time. Joanne was providing me efficiency stats ("We can produce 330,000 Goos Goos per day. Today, we'll do 10,000 boxes. That's an entire truckload . . ."). But I was watching the Latin women and thinking of this one photo of the Hershey's factory from back in the twenties, all these female immigrants sitting around a table foiling Kisses by hand. Bring us your huddled masses! We've got candy that needs wrapping!

The peanut-roasting room was our next destination. It featured an industrial roaster of the same sort I'd seen at Goldenberg, along with a giant IV bag type thing hanging from the ceiling. It was, bizarrely, filled with caramel.

Joanne turned to me. "Do you like coconut?" she said.

"Coconut," I said quietly.

"Oh, I just love coconut! Let's go see how we make our Coconut Haystacks!"

There was no time for questions, or excuses. Joanne had hustled me into a warm room that reeked of coconut. On the far side was a machine I recognized as a depositor. A worker was dumping what looked like corn chowder into the hopper at the top of the depositor. Down below, this batter was blorping out onto pans covered with waxed paper. The idea, I gathered, was for the batter to be drawn up to a point, like a Hershey's Kiss, or, more remotely, a haystack. But the consistency was far too watery. As they trundled away from the depositor, the haystacks flattened out into disks.

"It's the beginning of the run," Joanne said. "So Anthony, our quality control manager, is trying to make sure we got the batch proportions right." Anthony was indeed staring at the coconut batter in a silent rage.

Joanne spotted a rack full of finished Haystacks.

"You should try one," Joanne said.

"I'm really kind of full," I said.

"Oh come on. Don't be a wuss."

She handed me a Haystack. To be honest, it did not look like a haystack. It looked more like a shrimp, though I will say that the thick shreds of coconut did suggest a certain Monet-inspired haylike consistency. I popped the thing into my mouth, pretended to chew, and did one of those TV-commercial smiles.

Joanne said, "Good, huh? I love how buttery they are."

I watched Joanne bite into a haystack of her own and waited for mine to dissolve. It was a long wait.

Our last stop was the fruit room, where Standard produced a chew called ABC Fruit Chomps, which were sort of like a cross between a Tootsie Roll and a Starburst. These were not in production, though the room still smelled strongly of various fruit flavorings, jugs of which sat atop a worn-looking batch roller. The factory was, in this sense, sort of like a giant game of Clue. Each room had its own name and its own potentially lethal weapon. (It was *Anthony* in the *Coconut Room* with the *Nut Applicator*.)

Joanne led me through the warehouse, gingerly stepping over palettes strewn on the ground. She seemed to know everyone in the factory and, more astonishing, they all seemed delighted to see her. I myself liked Joanne, despite the fact that she had, more or less, force-fed me coconut. She had a firm grasp on the function of the basic factory machinery and used words such as *gunky* and *wuss*. The only dispute we got into was over how many Goo Goos I should take home with me. She felt I should take three boxes of six. I argued for two. "You can give them to the flight attendants on the plane," she said, pressing the third box on me.

"You're a *bad* person," I said.

"I *am* a bad person," she said coyly.

"You're suggesting that I bribe the flight attendants."

"I'm doing no such thing."

Her office was overflowing with promotional materials, so we settled into the conference room. I had noticed, on the way back, a big in-store display featuring a pile of candy bars I had never heard of before. These were brightly wrapped bars with generic sounding names which (somewhat predictably) Joanne asked me not to divulge.

Joanne explained that these were knockoffs of brand-name bars that Standard manufactured for a dollar store chain, which, in turn, sold them four for a dollar. Joanne assured me that these bars were often just as good as the brand-name products they mimicked. Having tried half a dozen of these bars, I must vigorously dissent. The Snickers rip-off, for instance, contained a mere smattering of peanuts and a thin band of caramel. Most of the bar was composed of a sickly sweet nougat that exuded a queer chemical aftertaste. Indeed, most of the bars suffered from the same unfortunate preponderance of corn syrup (as opposed to sugar) and dearth of chocolate. They were fascinating to sample, however, because they illustrated just how particular our taste in candy bars is. Although we rarely give it any conscious thought, we are acutely aware of just how many peanuts a Snickers should have, how thick the chocolate coating should be, what flavor the nougat ought to exude. And any deviations from this formula are glaring. Our taste buds are a finely calibrated instrument. The same was true of the ABC Fruit Chomps. They tasted funny. But they tasted funny because my palette has come to define Starbursts as the standard of normalcy when it comes to fruit chews.

I asked Joanne, point-blank, if Standard could survive without the contract work. She shook her head. Goo Goos had a nice mystique. They were a solid nostalgia item, and they did make some money, but not enough to keep the business going. Like officials at other smaller candy companies, Joanne lived in fear of a price war between the Big Three. She had already seen several regional candy companies go under, including Brock of Chattanooga, where she got her start.

Slotting fees were another issue. Standard generally couldn't afford to pay them, which had limited Goo Goo distribution to a variety of smaller grocery chains and alternative venues such as Dollar General and Cracker Barrel. They had no regular presence in Wal-Mart, the industry giant. And there was little chance, Joanne conceded, that they would ever expand north, beyond their core market. This was sad. It was sad to see a distinguished old company, with a rich history and a sensational (if sloppy) candy bar, reduced to cranking out diet bars and off-brands. But they didn't have the money to expand the market for Goo Goos. This was the bottom line.

Before the mood could turn too lachrymose, Joanne asked

me if I wanted to meet Jimmy Spradley, the president of the company. I didn't really want to meet Jimmy Spradley, but I figured it would be best if I said yes, so I did and Joanne led me to a large office just beyond the lobby. Jimmy was on the phone. His hair was slicked back and he was wearing a suit that looked like it cost more than my entire wardrobe. He took one look at me, in my wrinkled oxford and khakis, and squinted. His expression conveyed the basic message: *This* is a journalist? I felt a little embarrassed on Joanne's behalf. It was the sort of moment that made me wish (momentarily) that I was a billionaire.

Joanne offered to drive me to the airport, but only after loading me down with Goo Goos and a pecan log she insisted would rock my world.

And I did, in fact, attempt to give away one of my boxes of Goo Goo Clusters to the flight attendants on my trip back. I waited until after they'd come by with beverage service, then snagged the friendliest looking of the crew, an older woman with a tired looking fusillade of auburn hair.

She listened to my spiel with a vacant smile. "Goo Goo whats?" she said finally.

"Clusters," I said. "Goo Goo Clusters. They're like the official candy bar of the South."

"Is that so?"

"They're really good." I pulled out the box from my carry-on bag and directed her gaze to the sumptuous looking photo.

"There's no more room in first class," she said.

"I don't want to move into first class," I said. "I just thought you guys, like the rest of the crew, might want a treat."

"A treat?" she said.

"Right."

"Oh, I'd like that, honey. I really would. But we're not allowed to accept gifts from passengers. They're really strict on that since 9/11."

FREAK RETENTIVE

While I have long been one to harbor emergency candy stashes, the infusion of Goo Goos left me with something more on the scale of a bomb shelter supply. This was an indisputably wonderful development, but gazing upon the entirety, which covered my kitchen table, had the curious effect of launching me backwards, into my childhood. As I have implied, I was something of a candy hoarder back then.

I can still remember my brother Dave establishing a candy collection in the top drawer of his dresser, which included a shoelace-thin variety of red licorice that came in a sort of spool, and several sticks of Big Buddy gum. Although I do recall contributing a significant portion of my life savings toward these purchases, I do not recall actually eating any of the candy. (In the spirit of historical verification, I recently broached this topic with Dave, who claimed "not to remember" what I was talking about, and further advised that I "move on.")

Nonetheless, my tendency toward hoarding was, as I see it now, an outgrowth of such dynamics. It was not that our parents deprived us of sweets, but that the hallmark of our brotherhood was, to a larger extent than any of us would like to admit, emotional withholding. Simply put: it was verboten to express affection for one another, to praise or to hug. We didn't even like to laugh at each other's jokes. Instead, we communicated through boyish, and often brutal, antagonisms. Because I felt deprived of love, I hoarded my one dependable source of self-love, which was candy.

My brothers mocked me incessantly for this—*tightwad* being the favored sobriquet—and I understood that these tendencies were shameful. I couldn't help myself, though. I remember, as a teenager, ordering a pizza with my own money and, in a fit of stoned stinginess, hiding a couple of slices under the blanket at the foot of my bed. I forgot about these slices almost immediately. It was only two weeks later, when my room began to reek of rancid mozzarella, that I recalled what I'd done. Instant karma.

As an adult, I've worked hard not to be a tightwad. I shower my friends with boxes of candy. I try not to quibble over tabs. But the old instincts die hard. Occasionally, when I split a dessert with someone, I can feel myself gauging their consumption, figuring if I've gotten what I deserve. And I'm never quite sure that my generosity is genuine, and not, in some way, compensatory. What I mean to suggest here is that the primal pleasures of candy tend to elicit primal impulses. For those of us who grew up in a state of emotional or material want, the freak retentive lurks below all our selfless gestures.

I feel compelled to note the reaction of my friend Eve when I brought her a Goo Goo from Nashville: She launched into a story about how her father used to order Terry's chocolates from a sweets shop in his native Ireland. He kept these in his bedroom and dispersed them only reluctantly to his three children. Eve's mother later confirmed this account and added that she, herself, was kept on a strict ration. She even remembered finding a moldy box of Terry's on top of the armoire, where her husband had hidden them years earlier. Curiously, Eve is married to Evan, the Pop Rocks black marketeer who uses his spit to bore the center from Whoppers. They have two radioactively cute children, Milo and Theodora, both of whom were huge fans of the Goo Goo (or at least very much enjoyed rubbing the melted chocolate on their cheeks) and both of whom will, I suspect, require years of therapy down the line.

8

IN THE BELLY OF THE FREAK

Long before I began to visit actual candy factories, I harbored elaborate fantasies about visiting candy factories. The earliest of these involved a vague plan to track down the company that had produced (and ceased producing) the epic Caravelle. I assumed the operation was located in northern California, where I had grown up, and that it was run by a kindly old gentleman named Guipetto with whom I could discuss my allegiance to the Caravelle, the truly special nature of that bar, and that he would be so moved by my account that he would tear up and nod and say, "You're right, dear boy. Caravelle is the best bar we ever produced. I've always known that. But the board of directors told me it wasn't making enough money. Well, damn those vulgarians all to hell! We're going to reintroduce the Caravelle!" Then he would lean over his desk and press a button on his intercom and bark: "Miss Swanson! Get in here. I need to dictate a memo. Pronto!"

This was my fantasy. In my fantasy, Mr. Guipetto said *pronto*.

As my knowledge of the candy landscape became a bit more refined, I shifted to a somewhat less crazy plan: I would embark on a cross-country Candy Fellowship. The idea was that someone (a charitable foundation underwritten by the American Dental Association perhaps) would pay for me to take a coast-to-coast trip with stops at every candy company along the way.

This was clearly ridiculous. At the same time, it had become obvious that trying to visit factories one at a time, then returning to Boston, was even more ridiculous. So I laid plans for a final assault on the chocolate underbelly of America.

My criteria were pretty exhaustive:

1. Does the company manufacture a regional candy bar?
2. Will they let me in?

I contacted half a dozen companies, four of which showed the poor judgment to extend me an invitation. These were, in order of appearance:

- Palmer Candy of Sioux City, Iowa (Twin Bing)
- Sifers Valomilk of Merriam, Kansas (Valomilk)
- Idaho Candy Company of Boise, Idaho (Idaho Spud)
- Annabelle Candy of Hayward, California (Big Hunk, Rocky Road, Abba-Zaba)

The itinerary ran like so: On Monday, I was to take a 6 A.M. flight out of Boston to Milwaukee, then on to Omaha. From Omaha, I would have to find my way up to Sioux City, Iowa, then back down to Kansas City. On Tuesday, I would fly from Kansas City to Boise, via Denver. On Wednesday, I would fly from Boise to San Francisco, spend Thursday in Hayward, then catch the red-eye back to Boston, via Chicago's Midway Airport, in time to get myself to the class I was teaching at Boston College on Friday at noon. To save money, I had purchased plane tickets from a fast-talking Indian woman named Shirley, who had managed to book me (at a total cost of $992) on four different airlines, none of which I recognized. A couple of the connecting flights had a perilous half-hour layover, an arrangement that, as Shirley explained in her courteous-though-severe accent, could not be avoided.

Why did I take this trip? There are obvious answers: the sense of adventure, the free candy, the camaraderie. I hoped to seek out other purebred candyfreaks, men and women who still made bars the old way, in small factories, and who did so not primarily for profit but out of an authentic passion for candy bars.

This all sounds fabulous. But it was only a part of the truth. The whole truth would have to include the fact that a depression had been building inside me for some months. My journey began in early November and by this time there was a good deal of November in my heart. I mean by this that my life had taken on a gradual aspect of grayness, matched by the clouds which hovered outside my windows and dispelled a wearying rain. The ancient sorrows had resurfaced—the loneliness, the creeping sense of failure—and I felt doomed by the oncoming winter, trapped in the clutter of my apartment, frantic to escape. So I allowed myself to hope, as I had in childhood, that the pleasures of candy would help me beat a path from my despair.

On the eve of my departure I discovered, in the course of packing, at midnight, that I had lost my driver's license. I spent the next four hours ransacking my apartment. If you had had the ill fortune to be walking past my house at 4 A.M., you would have encountered a curious sight: a thin, anguished-looking man hunched inside a battered Toyota Tercel, lighting matches one by one, in a hopeless final attempt to locate his license. This was me, shivering in my bathrobe and weeping a little.

THE UNSTOPPABLE FREAK ENERGY OF MR. MARTY PALMER

The irony of the situation is that I lost my driver's license at the Arlex Driving School, where I had come for an all-day driver retraining course at the behest of the Registry of Motor Vehicles.

The alternative was to surrender my license and go to jail. But that's another story. The point is that I arrived in Omaha, after a lovely sunrise layover in Milwaukee, with two hours of sleep under my belt and no clear idea of how I was supposed to reach Sioux City, 100 miles north. I'd been able to board my flights with a passport. But no one was going to rent me a car without a license. I spent fifteen minutes loitering around the rental car desks, asking various terrified midwesterners if they were heading to Sioux City. They were not.

Eventually, I headed to the bathroom, and I mention this only because I saw in that bathroom the most quintessentially American artifact I have ever encountered: a bright blue rubber mat resting in the bottom of the urinal emblazoned with the following legend:

EPPLY
WORLD'S CLEANEST AIRPORT
OMAHA, NE

God bless our relentless idiotic optimism.

What did I do? I found an airport travel agent who informed me that there was a shuttle to Sioux City. My driver was a man named Bill who looked a great deal like Phil Donahue—the same big square face and snowy helmet of hair—if you can imagine Phil Donahue in a state of perpetual road rage. Bill had a voice like a coffee grinder. He had served in the military since Vietnam. When I asked him in what capacity, he responded, "Let's just say I was defending the interests of our country, alright?"

Oh, alright.

We bombed north up I-29, the cruise control set to 77 miles per hour. It was a bright, cold day and the sun beat down on fields of hacked cornstalks. "Feed corn," Bill said. "That's most of the business around here. It's all subsidized. You also got some pork futures. Those are pig farms. Only they don't like to say pig farms. It sounds degrading."

As we approached Sioux City, a giant refinery rose up on the right. This was Morrell, the meat company. The slaughtering, Bill informed me, was done at night. He often made late runs to the airport and assured me that the stench was overpowering, "a urine/fecal type stench."

It occurred to me that Bill wasn't necessarily what the chamber of commerce had in mind when it came to promoting the greater west Iowa basin. Then again, I had dated a woman from Sioux City and she made a great point of noting that the acronym for the Sioux City airport is SUX. It seemed to be that kind of place—prone to self-denigration.

Palmer Candy was located in a squat, brown brick warehouse on the western fringe of downtown. Marty Palmer himself met me at the door. He looked like an anchorman, tall, athletic, excellent teeth, and he was superfriendly in that guileless midwestern fashion that always makes me feel guilty for thinking such lousy things about the world. Marty had a total can-do attitude and no apparent neuroses and I didn't like him so much as I wanted, instantly, to *be* him. He was also, at 45, about 20 years older than he looked. (I found this to be a consistent attribute among the folks I visited; working with candy appeared to keep them preternaturally young.)

"I think they're doing the Twin Bings right now," Marty said. "So why don't we head into the factory and take a look?"

It is difficult to explain a Twin Bing to those who've never eaten one, because they are so spectacularly unlike other bars. Imagine, if you will, two brown lumps, about the size of golf balls, roughly textured, and stuck to one another like Siamese twins. The lumps are composed of crushed peanuts and a chocolate compound. Inside each of the lumps is a bright pink, cherry-flavored filling.

The filling, Marty explained, was actually a combination of two ingredients: nougat and fondant. Nougat, which contains egg whites, is fluffy. Fondant is a heavier, taffylike substance composed of sugar, corn syrup, and water. Together, they compose a cream. Marty made this quite clear as he led me into the brightly lit Cream Headquarters: I was to refer to the center of a Twin Bing as a *cream*.

He pointed to a circular steel table about two feet off the ground. "This is called a ball beater. It's where we prepare our fondant." The ball beater was not one of your more sophisticated machines. It had a set of giant plows that went round and round at about two miles per hour, so that, technically, it didn't really *beat* the fondant so much as shove it around. Eventually the fondant, which began as a viscous fluid, began to crystallize and thicken. At this point, a young guy hunched over the beater and pulled off hunks with his bare hands. Because the fondant was so sticky, he kept having to dip his hands in a pail of water. From a distance, he appeared to be heaving fish from a giant frying pan. Across the way, an industrial mixer was whipping up a batch of nougat. The two ingredients were blended in a giant kettle, along with the flavor and coloring. The result, a bright pink syrup, was then loaded into a depositor and squirted into molds. Marty and I stood watching a batch of cream centers being flipped from their molds and dropped into small white buckets, which were carried up an elevator and zipped into the next room.

Overseeing all this was a friendly older gentleman with a giant whisk in his hand. This was Paul, the Cream Center Manager. He had been working at Palmer from the time he was 18 years old. He was now 75. "I've hired five or six guys who were hoping to take over as manager, but Paul keeps going strong," Marty said.

Paul smiled shyly. "Well, everyone needs a little exercise," he said.

In the next room, a thousand cream centers had been piled into a glorious pink mountain. The centers, which looked like supersized gumdrops, were being directed onto a conveyor belt and carried under a curtain of chocolate coating. Next to this assembly line were two rows of women at workstations. Each woman had a stainless steel slab in front of her, shaped like a school desk. On these desks were two things: several dozen finished centers, now sheathed in a thin brown coat of chocolate, and a pile of chunky brown—well, what was it?

"That's called hash," Marty said. "It's a combination of crushed peanuts and chocolate compound."

These women (the Bingettes?) each held ice cream scoopers, which they plunged into the hash with one hand while, with the other, they pressed a center into the middle of the scoop. This caused an overflow of hash, which they smoothed down with a single, elegant backhand swipe. It was this swipe that covered over the cream center and created the flat bottom of the bar. The entire process took about two seconds. The finished Bing was then plopped onto a slowly moving assembly line. Another Bing was quickly set beside the first, close enough that they would stick together after being cooled.

"As far as we know, we're the largest handmade candy bar left in America," Marty said. "I know it's ridiculous, but there's really no other way to do it. Hash is very hard to work with, because it doesn't really flow. You can't really extrude it. You can't run it through an enrober. You have to handle it by hand. But that's alright, because we're having a good time using our hands." He looked up cheerily, as if he expected his workers to sing out their accord in unison. But these women were grim and otherwise absorbed. Their white smocks and blue rubber gloves were stained brownish red with hash, like field surgeons fresh from the front.

Marty's feelings about the Bing ran deep and sentimental. It was the most direct link to his legacy. The bar was introduced by his great-grandfather William Palmer in 1923, during the height of the candy bar craze. Of the original flavors (vanilla, maple, pineapple, and cherry) only cherry proved popular enough to survive. "We use the same wrapper my great-grandfather did," Marty explained, as we watched the Bings emerge from the cooling tunnel. "The Bing is the one thing we never mess with."

This was not entirely true. A couple of years ago, Marty introduced a Peanut Bing. But the combination of the peanuts in the hash and the peanut center "was just too much peanut for people," so Marty looked for another flavor. The result was the Crispy Bing, which features crisped rice around a peanut-flavored caramel cream center.

It is worth asking, at this point, how the Twin Bing actually tastes. The answer here is somewhat complicated. I found the bar disappointing initially. The compound had a waxy feel; it lacked the inimitable kick of real chocolate, the richness of the cocoa butter. The hash wasn't sweet enough. The whole crushed-peanut thing was weird—I was used to full or half nuts myself, and had come to assume the pleasure of grinding them up with my teeth. The cream center was too sweet, and its consistency was disorienting: heavier than a nougat, but chewier than a cream. This is to say nothing of the bar's appearance. And here I think it might be best to quote a friend of mine's nine-year-old son, who took one look at the Twin Bing and said, "What are those, gorilla balls?"

What I can't quite explain is how the bar managed to beguile me. It was sort of like that girl at the party who's so strange looking you can't stop thinking about her, until you realize that, despite all indications of good sense, you sort of dig her. This is what happened with me and the Bing. I ate a second bar purely to confirm my initial distaste. But after the third bar, and the fourth, there was no such excuse. I had begun to relish (secretly) the salty zest of the peanuts, the sugary bite of the cream center, which called to mind cherry bubble gum. In the end, what charmed me about the Bing was the melding of fruit and nuts, which is so rare among mass-produced candy bars. (I had high hopes for the Crispy Bing, because the bar bore an obvious similarity to the Caravelle. But the crisped rice hash lacked the desired snap, and the chocolate compound, without the rescuing bouquet of the peanuts, tasted like, well, compound.)

Marty was done with the Bing part of the tour. We were only getting started, though. Rather than taking the lean-and-mean approach of the Goldenbergs or relying on contract work—an honest but inevitably degrading arrangement—Marty had created a general line house of the old variety.

He marched me upstairs to the brittle room. Marty, I should note, was in sensational shape. He walked with that springy, pigeon-toed gait favored by ex-jocks. I figured he'd played soccer. "We didn't have soccer here when I was growing up," he said. "But I did run cross-country and I swam and raced sailboats."

The main thing Marty wanted to emphasize about his brittle was that the peanuts should be floating in the middle, which could only be achieved by a precisely timed hand-stretching of the brittle. Baking soda caused the brittle to aerate, or, in laymen's terms, to *puff up real fast,* so fast that I was briefly afraid the kettle being prepped would overflow and my shoes would be singed off by molten brittle. Instead, a couple of gloved workers grabbed the kettle and hoisted it over their heads and raced down the length of a cooling table, pouring the liquid brittle as they went. Now a flurry of activity began: one worker flattened the brittle with boards, a second, trailing behind, cut the brittle into squares, or hides, another flipped these over.

"See! The peanuts are starting to sink!" Marty explained.

"What these guys are going to do is stretch the brittle, which lifts the peanuts up. If they wait too long, it'll harden up." In the 30 seconds Marty had taken to explain the process, the workers had finished. Marty stepped to the table and broke off a piece of brittle and held it very close to my face. "See," he said. "Floating!"

Was Marty maybe going a little overboard on the floating peanut thing? Sure. But this was how he differentiated his product from the dozens of other brittles on the market. And more so, the story he told about his brittle was, in a sense, the story he was telling about himself. He was a craftsman. He regarded attention to detail as sacred. He took me to examine the copper kettles he used (the same kind as his grandfather) and the huge, scary peanut roaster, where redskins tumbled hypnotically around a bank of blue flame. He showed me the likewise huge and scary peanut fryer, which looked oddly like an ice cream cooler. Most of all, Marty wanted to emphasize the utmost importance of using these ingredients in an expeditious manner, to keep the "nutmeats from oxidizing" and becoming rancid. (I found myself repeating the word *nutmeat* for several weeks afterwards.)

As it should happen, we followed the fried peanuts downstairs, to the enrobing room on the first floor. Here, they were funneled into tiny metal baskets about the size of quarters. These baskets trudged along a conveyor belt and into a machine that drenched them in milk chocolate then lifted them off the conveyor belt, allowing the excess chocolate to drizzle off. This process—one I watched in a state of rapture for several minutes—created a spiffy little circular cluster. I have never been especially fond of peanut clusters, which always seemed a bit dry to me. Now I know why: because I had never eaten a cluster with *fried* peanuts.

On the line next door to the clusters, pretzels were being drenched in peanut butter. Another line had just finished a batch of pretzels enrobed in yogurt, with red and green Christmas drizzles. After Nestlé, Palmer was the nation's largest producer of coated pretzel products. Actually, Marty couldn't say this for sure, because there are no government statistics on coated pretzel products. But he was pretty sure.

The chocolate for all this coating came from a 60,000-pound vat in the basement. It was pumped upstairs, into an elaborate system of overhead pipes, then dumped into kettles for tempering. In the old days, Marty said, his staff had done all this by hand: broken the chocolate, melted it down, and slopped buckets from station to station. I found myself imagining a kind of Oompa Loompa free-for-all, with creepy green-and-orange dwarfs skating across floors slick with chocolate. It was not a pleasant vision.

"What do you mean by the 'old days,'" I said. "Like, the fifties?"

Marty laughed. "Oh no, our new chocolate delivery system is six years old."

In the repackaging department, a tall, ornate machine with steel pincers fed bulk candies into two-for-a-buck sacks. Repackaging, Marty explained, was another way for his company to eke out some profit. We watched batch after batch of gummy bears drop down onto the electronic scales.

When we got back to his office, I assumed Marty would tell me some heartwarming tale of visiting the factory as a kid and vowing someday to run the show. In fact, after high school Marty went off to the University of Colorado and spent five years there, collecting two degrees, one in engineering, the other in business. He interviewed with several companies after college. "I viewed the family business as an overgrown candy shop," Marty said. "It wasn't like: 'Boy, I'd like to come out of college and run *that.*' It was just a funky little deal."

Then fate intervened. Or, well, maybe not fate. More like a management crisis. The two gentlemen running the candy company retired. They had assumed Marty *would* return home to take over. Or, more precisely, that he would return home to oversee the sale of the business: "People figured we were just going to let it go under and milk it for what we could." Marty decided to do just the opposite.

When I asked him if he'd studied the recent history of the

candy industry, and specifically the gradual extinction of smaller companies, he nodded eagerly. "Yeah, I didn't care. I realized there was huge growth possible and there was going to be risk to it, but it *could* work, if we were willing to work hard. And the reason was this: the bigger the big guys get, the bigger the crumbs they leave on the table. Because frankly, if you're Mars or Hershey's, you don't even want to bother with a $10 million line." Marty paused and smiled broadly. "Well, *I* can make a fat lunch on that."

Marty knew that the Twin Bing was his flagship product. There were similar products on the market, such as the Cherry Mash down in Missouri, and the Mountain Bar, out in the Northwest. Bings dominated the ten northern midwestern states. His first impulse was to maximize sales within that zone. But the Bing, as it turned out, was already doing pretty well. It was the number four bar, for instance, in South Dakota. The real problem was that *no one lived in South Dakota*. Marty had a grand total of 5 million people within 400 miles of his plant. So he realized pretty quickly that he was not going to keep the lights on only doing Twin Bings.

Instead, he looked back at the history of the business, which his great-great-grandfather Edward Cook Palmer began, back in 1878, as a wholesale grocery. Edward's son, William, had made the move into candy at the turn of the century. Back then, Palmer was a general merchandise house. This was the strategy Marty adopted. His logic was simple: If you're a retailer, you only want to buy from one candy guy.

Marty was not blind to the realities of competing against companies a thousand times his size. But his tone conveyed the unmistakable swagger of an underdog who gloried in the odds against him. It occurred to me, as I watched him lean across his desk to emphasize his points, that he had probably been a very good athlete. "When we go knock on the door of the buyer, one of our biggest strengths is that we're *not* Mars or Hershey's. These guys say, 'Geez, you guys are the old style aren't you? Just making a go of it. That's great!' They'll look right at me and say, 'You can't really pay a $20,000 slotting fee, can you? How about $5 off the first 100 cases?' So we play let's make a deal. I truly believe, if a buyer is faced with a pretty level field and if it's close on cost they'll buy from me, because they've got an American flag tattooed on their heart."

This wasn't to say that Marty hadn't felt the squeeze of the Big Three. The example that leaped to mind was his chocolate-covered pretzel. For years, it had been a strong seller. Then Nestlé came along with Flipz. They spent millions of dollars in advertising to establish a national brand, and they took away a lot of Marty's business. The battle for seasonal sales had been vicious, as well. "The big guys can always come in and say: 'Would you like a better price on your everyday Butterfinger? Okay, but you need to buy fifteen items from us. How about if you buy this Butterfinger in a Christmas wrapper?' They can bring the power of their other brands to bear, because retailers can't live without Snickers or M&M's." Marty didn't sound bitter about any of these practices. Hell, they were simply good business. Such competitive disadvantages only made him more determined to turn Palmer into a regional powerhouse.

Over the years, Marty had received a lot of offers from people who wanted to buy the business, or a portion of it. It was their assumption that Palmer, as a small, independent candy company, was on its last legs. Marty's standard response was to agree to sell the business if the potential buyer agreed to pay him what he knew the business was going to be worth in ten years. He would then provide an estimate—rather a large estimate—and the buyer would, often in a state of pique, demur. Marty enjoyed these exchanges a great deal. They were one of the dividends of his hard work.

Another was the chance to produce—or, at least, to fantasize about producing—new products. He realized that kids these days were more interested in handfuls of things and sours. But Marty himself favored "the old soldiers," vanished candy bars of yesteryear. His most cherished dream was to reintroduce a bar called the Walnut Crush, which had been made by the Fenn Brothers, up in Sioux Falls, 100 miles north. "That was a delicious bar," Marty said, a little dreamily. "It was kind of like a 3 Musketeers, but the filling was bright white and it had a walnut flavor and a different texture, what we call 'short,' which is a baking term, meaning that it bites off cleanly, it doesn't pull. It was covered in dark chocolate. A very unusual piece."

The Fenn Brothers went out of business in the early seventies. When Marty took over, he tracked down the old formula and found a few former employees, who described how they made the Walnut Crush: laying the centers on cookie sheets and drying them for three days. That process had given the Crush its distinct snap, but it also made the bar impossible to mass produce, at least profitably. Marty's heart seemed to sink a little at the memory.

He was, after all, being asked (or asking himself) to play two conflicting roles simultaneously: Guardian of the Past and Forward-Thinking Business Owner. This duality was apparent everywhere, in his business decisions, in the factory's mishmash of new and old equipment, even in the decor of his office, which included a sleek computer as well as a framed piece that I'd been eyeing curiously. It appeared to be an aged strip of cloth stitched with the Palmer name, along with the legend DELICIOUS CHOCOLATES SOLD HERE. "Actually, that's a branded calfskin," Marty said. This was a nod to Sioux City's legacy as a leader in the meat industry. Back at the turn of the century, Palmer delivered its candies as far as a horse-drawn wagon could travel in a day. These wagon jobbers would often nail a calfskin sign to a post out front of the dry goods stores they visited. "These guys were the Bud signs of their day." He had framed his.

He had a lot of other relics, too, stuff he couldn't quite bring himself to throw out, though he knew he probably should. "It is nice to have a little history around," he said, almost apologetically. "It helps you remember where you came from. My grandfather used to come in all the time to chew the fat. He told me about this promotion they used to run for a boxed chocolate product called Lucky Day, or Golden Strike, something having to do with luck. What he would do is cook up a batch of 300 pounds of soft nougat and throw a handful of gold coins into the batch and then of course they'd be made into candy. As a consumer, you knew you might get a piece of gold. You'd get arrested today for doing things that used to be good marketing." Marty shook his head.

While we'd been talking, a secretary had appeared and placed a box of chocolate pretzels and clusters on his desk. These were my parting gifts. We climbed into his SUV, which was about the size of my apartment, and cruised toward town.

Sioux City is best known, historically, as the starting point of Lewis and Clark's westward expedition. There is a large, phallic monument not far from the Morrell plant commemorating the explorers, as well as a business park environment named after them. In fact, Sioux City had been the biggest town between Chicago and Denver at the dawn of the twentieth century. But then someone had paid off someone else and the railroad had gotten routed through Omaha and Sioux City had gone into a steady decline.

The city was enjoying a renaissance, though, in part due to Gateway, which had come to town and brought 7,000 jobs. Marty cited the restoration of the Orpheum Theater, where he had gone the previous evening to see *Riverdance.* The city was also hard at work on a 10,000-square-foot events center. Marty was especially pleased by this project, because it was being built right next to the old Palmer factory, the first floor of which was still being used as a candy shop. We paid the shop a brief visit so Marty could show me the cracks in the tiled floor, the result of two errant boxcars which, back in 1931, bounded across the street and crashed into the front of the building.

Just before he dropped me off at the Greyhound bus station, I asked Marty if he ever questioned the decision he'd made to return to Sioux City. He said no, not really, that he realized the place wasn't Paris, but this is where his factory was and he felt a responsibility toward the 100 workers he employed. He had no delusions about the future. "It would be neat to have a sixth generation," he said, gazing at the fleet of gantry cranes that loomed over his downtown. "But you never know what kids will want to do." It seemed to me, in that moment, that Marty Palmer was straddling the two worlds that compose our lives, the past and the present, with tremendous grace.

SOUTHBOUND WITH THE HAMMERS DOWN

So I left Marty riding a high of borrowed optimism. Great things seemed possible. What I needed was a positive attitude, an appreciation of my own history, a sense of possibility. This lasted 23 minutes.

I was four hours early for my bus, so I wandered down Sixth Street, past the hospitals, toward the wide and muddy Missouri River. Sioux City reminded me of El Paso, weirdly, because of the various down-in-the-mouth Mexican restaurants, but also because of the low-slung dustiness of the place, the proximity of a strong-smelling industry (in El Paso it was lard), and the general sense of lassitude. It even looked like El Paso on a map: the convergence of three states around a river. North Sioux City was actually in South Dakota. South Sioux City was in Nebraska. Neither of these states, thankfully, had felt it necessary to post guards at their border. Last of all, there was the bus station itself, which I initially mistook for an abandoned dwelling. It was a fantastically grim little spot at the top of a ragged bluff, full of tired, yellow air.

I thought about the rental car I might have been driving, had I not lost my driver's license, had I not hated myself quite so much, had I grown up in a different family, one with a finer appreciation for the simplicities of love. By now, just after four, I'd be on the outskirts of Kansas City already, checking into a hotel room, settling into a bath, with one of the *Rocky* pictures blaring on cable.

But I was, instead, in a gravel lot, shivering alongside a group of passengers with duffel bags and battered plastic sacks. If you ever want to know what America really looks like—and I direct this chiefly toward the residents of the coastal cities who tend to write about America most frequently—I would suggest you abandon the airports. The only people in airports are rich people. Take a bus from Sioux City to Kansas City, via Omaha and Maryville. Here is where America lives, more often than not overweight, beset by children, fast-food fed, television-dulled, strongly perfumed, running low on options and telling their stories to whomever will listen, hatching schemes, self-dramatizing, preaching doomed sermons, dreaming of being other people in other lives.

The woman next to me, thickly shadowed about the eyes, munching on a fried fish sandwich, told me she'd been in Sioux City for the weekend, up from Council Bluffs to visit her boyfriend, who hadn't seemed to love her so well when they were living in the same town, had even mistreated her, but was now pledging undying love, had asked her to move in actually, and even proposed marriage, though without a ring.

"I'm waiting for the ring," she said.

"That sounds like a good idea," I said.

I thought about my own romantic history, such as it was. I'd been no better than this fellow in most cases—a little slicker, maybe, a little cagier. My last serious girlfriend had been the woman from Sioux City. She was the one who had turned me on to the Twin Bing, a few months before I politely bailed on her. Recently, she'd sent me an e-mail to let me know she was getting married, and this note, more than I liked to admit, had contributed to my blue mood. It occurred to me that I was envious of my neighbor. She was, at least, engaged in that most human of struggles, toward love, while I was playing it safe in solitude, keeping my hands busy, my heart on ice.

The bus hurtled on toward Omaha, where we took an hour break. The station there was bigger, full of ancient video games and vending machines, a bacterial snack bar, and crowded with people in an amped state of transit. The kids were running wild as a response to all the anxiety and their parents were overdoing the discipline—tears, recrimination, the white-hot building blocks of future arrests. On the grainy TV overhead, an anchorwoman was waxing eloquent about the next day's elections. Her demeanor suggested the basic message: *Isn't democracy neat?* Democracy is neat. The notion that the poor man's vote counts as much as the rich, that the poor might band together in order to choose benevolent leaders; this is as neat as civilization gets. But you would have never known that the election had anything to do with the people gathered in that station.

Outside, in the cold clear night, an old man, drunk to the point of disorientation, kept trying to board the bus. When the driver approached him, he would back away, hands up, and mutter into his sleeve. There was a family of six, no dad in sight, who seemed to be moving their entire estate south, suitcase after battered suitcase, even the little ones with their load to bear, midwestern refugees.

The driver for the second leg of our trip was a jovial fellow who looked like Ichabod Crane and sounded like Louis Armstrong, a combination I found disorienting. "Howdy back there," he growled into his intercom. "We're headed southbound with the hammers down. So just re-lax and leave the driving to yours truly."

All around us, darkness was coming to the plains. The children were settling down to sleep and a few adults were murmuring in their little cones of light. I tried for sleep, but the night had called my anxiety out of hiding. I could feel it rippling my stomach, whispering its ancient incantations. *You are unworthy of love. Candy will not save you.* We barreled south into Missouri and detoured at Maryville, through a freak hailstorm that clattered off the roof of the bus and frightened the children from their dreams.

9

THE CANDY BAR ON YOUR CHIN

At nine the next morning a white van emblazoned with the orange-and-brown Sifers Valomilk logo pulled up to my hotel. Russ Sifers hopped out. He was wearing a white sweatshirt, also decorated with the Valomilk logo, and matching brown corduroy pants. "This is what I wear to work every day," he announced. "You look in my closet, it's pretty boring. Five pairs of cords, five sweatshirts. I'm at a point in my life where I can be very laid-back. I'm not out to set the world on fire."

This was not entirely true. Despite running what was, by any standard, a tiny operation, Russ Sifers had generated a massive amount of press, in part because he had a good story to tell and in part (as I would discover over the next few hours) because he so relished telling it.

Russ had the sort of face that makes for an excellent mall

Santa, ruddy and full-cheeked. He even wore the requisite gold-rimmed spectacles. He moved deliberately and spoke in a Missouri twang so slow as to suggest a kind of theatrical folksiness. When he related a story, which was often, he acted out his own role in an exaggerated version of this sodbuster accent. "Got an e-mail this morning from a lady who can't find Valomilks in Des Moines," he told me, as we sped north toward his factory. "So I'm gonna have to check that out when I get home. No computers in the office, course. I tell folks we're computer-free. No PDAs, no beepers, no cell phones, though we do have an electric typewriter with correction ribbon."

Russ pulled up in front of a small building with a flagstone façade. It did not look like a factory. In fact, the building had housed a day-old bakery before Russ rented it out fifteen years ago. He checked the production schedule taped to the wall outside his office. It listed each day, followed by the word *cook* or a blank space. The inventory as of that day was one box. When Russ told people that Valomilks were made to order, he meant it.

His office had the feel of a museum. A copper kettle stood in one corner, along with antique bottles of vanilla, candy molds, yellowed ads, photos, mixing spoons, and punchboards. Sifers was one of the first candy companies to produce punchboards, and one of the last. Russ's grandfather, Harry, had nearly gotten himself arrested for selling them, because they were considered gambling.

A framed photo above the kettle showed the company's headquarters, circa World War II, a stately building rising from the heart of downtown Kansas City. When people asked Russ how long he'd been in the candy business, he always told the same story, how on Easter morning 1948, his mother brought him down to the factory. Russ was in a basket and his proud grandfather toted him around, boasting to all his employees, "This is the heir apparent to the company." For a long time, Russ figured this was just his mom, telling a quaint little Moses-and-the-bulrushes-type story. Then, one day, he received a letter from a former employee. "Dear Russ," it began, "I'll never forget the day your grandfather brought you around the factory in that Easter basket." To Russ, this story had acquired the semimystical power of a creation myth: he was born to make candy.

The Sifers family began producing confections in 1903 in Iola, Kansas, before moving the business north to Kansas City. Russ's great-grandfather Samuel Mitchel Sifers was one of the most prolific figures of the candy bar boom, creator of such delicacies as the Old King Tut, Subway Sadie, Ozark Ridge, Rough Neck, Jersey Cow, Snow Cup, and the KC Bar.

The Valomilk didn't come along until 1931. Like many of the most famous candy bars, it was the result of a snafu. Back in those days, vanilla had a high alcohol content and, as the legend goes, Sifers employed a candy maker named Tommy who'd been hitting the vanilla pretty hard. He was supposed to make a batch of marshmallow, but it came out all runny. Harry was always looking for new ideas for candy, so he put scoops of the runny marshmallow in milk chocolate cups. The Valomilk (the name is a rough amalgam of the ingredients) was an instant hit. Russ's father later introduced a chocolate version, and a crunchy Valomilk, with toasted coconut, followed soon after. "My dad was liable to experiment," Russ explained. "People write me sometimes and say, 'Why don't you make the Crunchy anymore?' My dad loved coconut. He's dead and gone. I hate coconut."

I told him I understood *completely*.

Russ graduated from Kansas University with a degree in business administration and went on to get certified as a candy technologist. There was never much doubt as to whether he'd join the family business. When his father retired in 1974, he took over at the ripe old age of 26. During the fifties, Sifers had been one of the most prominent candy concerns in the Midwest. But by the time Russ came along, the business had been bought out by Hoffman, a Los Angeles–based company that produced a similar marshmallow cup called the Cup-O-Gold. They had grand plans, to consolidate and go national. In effect, though, Hoffman was an absentee owner. The arrangement "didn't work worth a hoot," Russ recalled. In ten years, the owners visited Kansas City a grand total of three times. In 1981, they opted to shut the Sifers factory down and the Valomilk disappeared from the candy landscape. Six years later, Russ decided to resurrect the company on his own, using equipment salvaged from the old plant.

Russ settled himself behind a vast mahogany desk. It, too, had been handed down from his grandfather. A Depression-era canvas banner hung on the wall behind him, advertising Valomilks at five cents a piece. Nearby was a map of the United States beset by colored push pins. These were intended to chart various aspects of Valomilk's distribution, though the system had been somewhat compromised by Russ's tendency to use dark blue pins, for instance, when he ran out of light blue ones.

Russ cocked his head. "You hear that?"

I didn't hear anything, just the dull roar of traffic. Then it came to me—a faint syncopated rhythm: ba-*bum*-ba-*bum*.

Russ smiled. "There's a real music to the line when it's up and running. Let's go see what they're doing."

Before we could do that, a young man in a blue uniform appeared and introduced himself as a fire inspector. "I was hoping to look around the premises."

"Sure!" Russ said. "Of course! You ever seen a candy factory? You'll love it."

He led us down a short hallway, which was (like much of the available office wall space) decorated with press articles about Valomilk, then outside, and then back inside through a second door. The ba-*bum* noise was now louder and more distinct: a sharp hydraulic hiss followed by a metallic ping.

To call the operation a factory is technically correct, but somewhat overstates the scale of things. It looked more like an industrial kitchen. Russ gestured toward a squat cylindrical machine, the chocolate melter. A worker opened the spigot and filled a small pail with chocolate, which he set about vigorously stirring. He allowed the chocolate to cool a bit, checked the temperature with a thermometer (which I very much wanted to lick), and began stirring again. It took me a moment to realize that he was actually tempering the chocolate *by hand*. This is almost unthinkably impractical—the rough equivalent of GM casting their bolts by hand. But it was typical of Russ's approach to candy making, which was attractively fanatical.

He was equally picky about ingredients, insisting on pure cane sugar, for instance, rather than beet sugar, and bourbon vanilla, which is grown exclusively on the island of Madagascar (formerly the Isle of Bourbon), the source of the world's finest vanilla beans. The vanilla cost Russ $200 per gallon. Years ago, Russ told me, he used spray-dried egg whites for his marshmallow. Then he heard a rumor about a slightly higher-quality product, pan-dried egg whites, and knew, at once, he had to have them. He started making calls and eventually found a gentleman at the American Institute of Baking, who told him there was only one company in the country that made pan-dried egg whites. Russ was so thrilled when he finally tracked them down that he rushed home to tell his wife. *Guess what, honey?* he said. *I just increased the price of our egg whites by 53 percent!*

We caught Roman, the head cook, in the midst of making a batch of marshmallow filling. On the table were six Tupperware bowls filled with pan-dried egg whites, which were being rehydrated—in distilled water, naturally. A large, gentle man with mournful eyes, Roman moved with superlative grace as he carried the egg whites across the room and poured them into a large mixer. In a matter of minutes, they were whipped into a snow-white meringue. Meanwhile, Roman prepared a concoction of corn syrup, sugar, salt, and vanilla, which he lugged over to a second mixer. The scent of bourbon vanilla suffused the room.

"This mixer is called a Hobart," Russ said. "I was using one of these when we first started and it broke down. I called the manufacturer to see if I could get the part I needed and they said, 'We haven't made parts for that since the fifties. What are you doing with that thing?' I said, 'I'm using it to make candy.' They couldn't believe it."

Roman turned the Hobart on and slowly eased the speed up. Then he went and got the egg whites and carefully folded them into the vanilla mixture. The result was a satiny white liquid that lipped over the edge of the bowl with every rotation of the blades but never quite spilled. The whole process looked deceptively simple. But that was how it often was with candy production. The perils were hidden. "You can't expose the egg whites to too much heat or they'll coagulate," Russ explained. "The other thing you have to watch for, if you try to speed up that mixer too quick you wind up covered in marshmallow. We learned that one the hard way."

Roman nodded. He returned to the table with the egg whites and bent down to record the details of the batch he'd just finished—not on a computer, but in a dog-eared business ledger.

I had never seen a cup candy being manufactured, though I had spent a good deal of time admiring the crinkled ridges of chocolate and thin walls and pondering how in the hell an automated machine could produce such an elegant shape. What happened was this: A depositor plinked liquid chocolate into each of the brown glassine cups. These cups then passed under a row of brass pipes, which let out a sharp burst of air, blowing the chocolate up and onto the sides of the paper cup. (It was the sound of this process that produced the distinctive hiss and ping I'd heard earlier.) The cups were blasted with cold air again, to solidify the chocolate. A foot later, the marshmallow syrup was deposited into the cups, coiling down snakelike and settling flat. Then, get this, *another* plink of chocolate was released onto the (now full) cup, producing a chocolate and marshmallow yin/yang design. I should mention that the young fire inspector was fascinated by this process. He spent a good two minutes watching the liquid chocolate rise up into the sides of the cup, a gorgeous sight to be sure, though probably not, in the grand scheme of things, a major fire risk.

But how, you might fairly ask, did this yin/yang design transform itself into a finished Valomilk? The answer was diabolically simple.

"We shake them," Russ said.

He led me into the next room, where workers were removing each rack of molds and shaking them in a distinct circular motion, so that the top layer of chocolate oozed down and around and connected to the rest of the cup. It was a process that didn't look that hard—imagine hula-hooping with a metal rack in your hands—until you considered that the chocolate only stayed liquid for a minute or so and that you had to worry about 30 different cups and make sure that all of them, no matter where they were positioned on the rack, got full chocolate coverage. If you allowed the chocolate to seep too far in any one direction, you were screwed. I stood and watched one woman tip the rack first one way, then the other, applying a gentle shake at fixed intervals, so as to coax the chocolate into place. The image called to mind the waning of 30 tiny, gibbous moons.

"When we first started doing this, it was a real mess," Russ said. "We had a ton of leakers. Of the three batches we tried, only one of them came out right."

There was no room for a cooling tunnel in the factory, so Russ had been forced to improvise, using a large, standing fan to blow cool air through the racks.

That was the whole process. The cups, once cooled, were set on a tiny conveyor belt and shuttled, two at a time, onto a strip of cardboard, which was then heat-sealed in an elegant plastic wrapper, a method of wrapping that went out of vogue more than three decades ago. "What I've done, basically, is taken our technology backwards. Most of this stuff is somewhere between forties and fifties technology. I spent weeks trying to imagine how to set up the factory. And when I got stuck, I asked myself: 'Now, how would my grandfather have done this?' "

Russ then asked me the question I was afraid he was going to ask me: Had I ever actually eaten a Valomilk?

I shook my head.

He squinted in distress, grabbed a freshly wrapped pack, and pressed it into my hands.

THE MARSHMALLOW PARALLAX

The truth is I'm not a huge fan of marshmallow. In fact, I sort of hate marshmallow. What I was hoping would happen is that I'd be able to slip the candy bar into my pocket and eat it later. But Russ led me back to his office and sat down and folded his arms across his chest. His expression was unmistakably smug. He looked like a major cocaine lord waiting for a new buyer to sample his goods. (Not that I am intimately familiar with the facial expressions of major cocaine lords.)

As I bit down into my first cup, I immediately understood why: the interplay of the chocolate and the vanilla syrup was astonishing. Until that moment, I had never understood the synergy between these two flavors. The pairing had just been a trope, to my mind, a cliché. But here, inside my mouth, it was finally dawning on me: the way in which the airy tones of vanilla infused the chocolate and lent the heavy tang of cocoa a sense of buoyancy. What I realized in that moment was this: it wasn't the *flavor* of marshmallow that bothered me so much as the texture, that fluffy, half-empty springiness. But the Valomilk filling was really more like the gooey center of a toasted marshmallow, though that's not quite right either, because the vanilla in a Valomilk is far more pungent than any mainstream marshmallow.

"The way we designed it is that you start with this burst of chocolate," Russ said. "Then you hit the filling and it's so sweet that it sort of overwhelms you for a while. Then the chocolate reemerges at the end and it gives the bar a great finish."

The only problem with the Valomilk involved what I want to call *oral logistics*. It was the single most difficult-to-eat candy bar I had ever encountered. No sooner had I taken my first bite, than the entire cup collapsed and the filling began to drip everywhere: onto the wrapper, onto my sweater, and, most prominently, onto my chin.

Russ chuckled. "You know the motto they used for Valomilk? When It Runs Down Your Chin, You Know It's a Valomilk. I did a lot of trade shows back when I was getting the business back up and running and I remember I was up in Topeka and these two women came to my booth. 'Oh, Valomilks!' one of them said. 'I remember those! They were like a little taste of heaven.' And the whole time she was talking to me, she was doing this thing." Russ began to rub at his chin absently. "She had no idea she was doing it. It was her memory that set it off."

This was all fine and well, but I was in a bit of a crisis, sweaterwise. So I took the entire cup, the sharded remains anyway, and shoveled them into my mouth.

I attacked the second cup more carefully, breaking off a portion of the chocolate lid and sipping at the syrup, demitasse style. Then, when Russ went off to say hello to his secretary, Mildred, I broke off the rest of the lid and used it like a tortilla chip to dip into the syrup. Then I went straight at the syrup with my finger. When I was left with just a film of filling, I popped the cup into my mouth.

Russ came back into his office. He took one look at me and got me a Kleenex and a bottle of water.

"Once you take that first bite, it's pretty much crisis management," Russ said. "I get mail all the time from people asking the right way to eat a Valomilk. I had one woman who wrote to tell me I almost caused her to have a car accident. She was trying to eat one while driving, which I don't recommend. She said she pulled over to the side of the road and while she was pulled over she ate the other cup, which she was supposed to be taking home to her husband. So then she had to turn around and go buy another one. My college roommate, Mark Dempsey, used to eat four, chased by a Diet Coke. Had one guy who worked at an auto salvage place who wrote to tell me my candy bar had almost ruined his cash register. I asked my daughter Sarah about this once, because she was studying child psychology. I said, 'Why are people so fascinated by how to eat Valomilks?' She said, 'Well, Dad, they're round and they're messy. But that's what makes them fun. Once we get older we're not supposed to be messy anymore. But for one moment when you're eating a Valomilk, it's okay to be messy again.' "

It goes without saying that I explored a number of methods,

using the supply of Valomilks Russ later foisted upon me, including but not limited to:

> *The Pin Prick:* Using the end of a relatively clean paper clip, I bored a hole in the bottom of the cup and let the syrup drip down into my mouth.
>
> *The Flip Top:* I broke off the top lid, in its entirety, and lapped at the filling with my tongue directly.
>
> *The Glutton:* Whole cup into my mouth. (Not recommended for diabetics.)

In a sense, the Valomilk is as antiestablishment as a candy bar can get. In recent years, the Big Three have sought ways to make the consumption of candy more and more convenient. They've come up with an endless variety of bite-size pieces, most individually wrapped. In so doing they've not just clogged the nation's landfills, but bled the act of candy consumption of its inherent, regressive joys. There is little sense of improvisation, let alone danger, when a piece of candy comes ready to eat.

The inconvenience of the Valomilk wasn't limited to consumption issues. It was also hard to transport. For one thing, Russ shipped his candy via UPS, in quantities usually no greater than a gross. He couldn't afford refrigerated trucks, so he was reluctant to ship anyplace where the temperature was likely to exceed 80 degrees. During the warm months, he watched the Weather Channel before coming into work and made a daily map of acceptable shipment sites. Finally Valomilks explode at high altitude.

"Well, they don't explode exactly," Russ said. "I just use that word to make it sound dramatic. But the filling does expand and they leak. The ones that don't have a leak already become little leakers and the little leakers become super leakers. You can't take them over the Rockies, or on a plane." Russ did not mention these limitations with any great measure of frustration. These were simply the radical conditions of doing business in the way he did. (I, however, am ready to express a certain measure of frustration, because I was left with no choice but to transport my box of Valomilks over the Rockies by plane, not once, but twice. By the time I got home, each and every one of the cups had sprung a leak and the filling had congealed into a Krazy Glue–like substance capable of great binding force, rendering it difficult, if not impossible, to remove a Valomilk from its paper cup. Not that this kept me from trying.)

Clearly, Russ Sifers considered candy a calling. But there had also been an element of chance behind his decision to start making Valomilks again. In 1985, he was driving to Manhattan, Kansas, for a parents' weekend at Kansas State, when a local radio host began talking about Valomilks. Russ listened in amazement as caller after caller lamented their disappearance. This was the era before cell phones, so he couldn't call the show, but he did write a letter, which the host read on the air the next week. This spurred another flood of calls. "I'd grown up around Valomilks and always kind of taken them for granted," Russ said. "This was the first time I'd realized how special they were to people."

Russ was working on the assembly line at GM at the time, but he continued to mull the idea of reviving Valomilks, even going so far as to present some handmade samples at a local chocolate festival. He didn't get serious until a couple of years later, when the absentee owners asked him if he'd be willing to clean out the old downtown factory, which they wanted to sell. Russ went by with a flashlight to scout it out. He found all the old equipment, still there in the coal room in the basement. "I had the strangest feeling looking at those machines," he said. " 'That's the stuff my grandfather used! There's the chocolate melter! I kind of remember I had to step up on a stool to see into that!" Russ knew GM was planning a round of layoffs, that the getting was good. All his kids had gone through college. His mission suddenly seemed obvious.

He agreed to clean up the building if he could keep the old equipment and the rights to the Sifers Valomilk name. He even got himself transferred to the night shift at GM so he could spend his days planning the relaunch. There were a hundred things to consider: how to rehab the equipment, where to find factory space, if the old recipes could even be reproduced.

"The first batch of filling nearly caused a divorce," Russ said. "My wife and I were making it in our kitchen and she said, 'How many cups of sugar should I put in?' I said, 'Well now, it was 200 pounds of corn syrup, 100 pounds of sugar.' She said, 'How many *cups*, Russ?' We about killed one another."

The chocolate was also a problem. The original Valomilks were made with a special chocolate bought from Hershey's called Sifers Triple A, a slightly darker milk chocolate, specially blended for creaminess. Russ contacted Hershey's to try to get the recipe. The call went unreturned. So he did what any obsessive would: he commissioned a local chocolatier to reproduce Sifers Triple A. To make sure he was getting the taste just right, he tracked down people who had eaten the bar in the thirties and began conducting independent taste tests with each of them. It took weeks for the tasters to concur that Russ had re-created the original recipe. He was right to be so thorough. The chocolate in the Valomilk was transcendent; I would go so far as to call it *velvety*.

After more than two years of concerted scheming, Russ began production. He liked to point out that he moved from the largest corporation in the world to the smallest, a true statement given that he didn't have any actual employees at inception. He had to beg folks to come in and work as volunteers after church, and pay them in rejects. Russ was so excited when he finished the first two boxes that he raced down to the distributor and announced, "Here they are! The Valomilks have arrived!" The distributor stared at him and asked for an invoice. "Oh yeah," Russ said, "I have to bill you for these, don't I?"

He soon began seeking distribution outside Kansas City. "One day I told my wife, 'I've got six cases and I'm not coming back till they're all sold.' That was two days' production back then." Russ drove from Lawrence to Topeka to Hutchinson and sold all six cases in one day. It turned out the distributors who had worked with his father and grandfather were happy to help. He sent a price sheet to one fellow in Missouri who called him back and agreed to stock Valomilks in his warehouses, all across the state. Russ hoped to make Valomilks available in every midwestern town; in the first, heady months of the business, this had seemed realistic.

It no longer does. "We can't do it," he told me. "Wal-Mart and Kmart and Targetmart and Whatevermart, they're in control of the marketplace. Take a place like Maryville, Missouri. There used to be four groceries in Maryville. Then Wal-Mart announced they were building a supercenter, 160,000 square feet. In a single year, three of those groceries have gone under and the last one's on the ropes. Now: I can't get into Wal-Mart. People still want Valomilks, but they're killing off the avenues we have to get our candy out there." Russ noted, with considerable disgust, that he'd been asked to pay $20,000 as a slotting fee by the Associated Wholesale Grocers. He was unable to.

As I listened to Russ, I could see my dream of a bunch of small, independent microconfectioners crumbling. The mass production of a candy bar required a huge initial investment with little chance of large-scale retail sales. Russ, after all, already had an established brand name. He knew the business. He'd gotten his equipment for free. And still, he was struggling.

"People say to me, 'Hey Russ, how's business doing?' I say, 'Better than Enron. Better than Worldcom.' What else am I going to say? I had some guy come in and try to sell me a business consulting plan. I said, 'I know we need more sales. I know we need to get in more stores. And I know those stores are disappearing.' I know the distributors are disappearing, too. I read their obituaries. Those are people who sold to my father and my grandfather. They're like a death in the family. And I've had enough of those." For a second, I didn't understand what Russ meant. Then I remembered something he'd told me earlier, in the factory, that his oldest daughter had succumbed to cancer in 1999.

From the next room, I could hear Mildred whacking at the keys of her electric typewriter. One of the workers appeared in the doorway, and Russ, lodged in an uncustomary silence, looked relieved at the interruption.

"How'd we do with the fire inspector?" he asked.

"Passed," the young man said.

Russ smiled. "This is Dave, our factory manager. He also happens to be my stepson Dave Swiercinsky. You're looking at the fifth generation."

Dave blushed a little.

"When the time comes, he'll inherit this desk," Russ announced. "In a sense, I view myself as a steward. That's a biblical term. It just means a caretaker. I don't really own the company. I'm just a caretaker. And when it comes time for me to move on, then Dave can take care of it."

Russ had assumed his tone of avuncular jocularity, but there was something unmistakably sad in the air. I felt I had overstayed my welcome. This being the Midwest, however, Russ insisted on driving me to the airport, after he took care of a couple of things. I spent the next few minutes in the office next door, chatting with Mildred, who told me she used to live in Boston with her late husband. Her husband had worked for a manufacturer of prosthetic limbs and the company used to send him out to show folks how to operate their new arms and legs.

"Was he an amputee?" I said.

"Oh yes," Mildred said. "Yes. I probably should have mentioned that. They paid all his expenses, motel and gas money and so forth. I would go along on weekends. We got to see a lot of the country that way."

The ride to the airport was dispiriting. The view from I-35 was mostly shopping centers. There were a few open lots where bulldozers were clearing the ground, presumably for more shopping centers. Russ provided a glum play-by-play of the development. We passed by the Missouri River. A factory on the far bank was coughing a thick plume of smoke into the clouds. Just before we reached the airport, Russ admitted that he'd been contacted by another candy company about the possible sale of his business. These were just discussions, he said quietly. There was nothing in writing. I was stunned. Just a few minutes ago, he'd sounded so committed to passing the business down to Dave.

I sat in the Kansas City airport, eating lousy barbeque and thinking about the strangeness of my visit. Russ had initially presented himself as a man without worries, a scrapper who'd made it against the odds. But the longer he talked, the less convincing he'd sounded. There'd been a real rage in his denunciations of Wal-Mart and the other corporate bullies. I wondered to what extent this rage was really about the larger injustice he'd suffered: losing his daughter. Most forms of rage, after all, are only sloppy cloaks for grief. I should make clear: Russ hadn't dwelled on her death. He'd focused on the factory he'd brought to life, the miraculous white of the marshmallow, the thick fragrance of hand-beaten chocolate. But tragedies of a certain magnitude bleed into everything.

As she got sicker, Russ told me, he'd turned his attentions toward her and her children, and away from the business. One afternoon she'd called him on the phone, told him she didn't feel well, and he'd raced over to her house to look after the kids. "I just wasn't focused on work," he said. He blamed himself, in part, for the recent downturn in revenues. This was a ludicrous notion. But it's the kind of thing survivors do all the time. They find a way to punish themselves for remaining alive.

I thought of how Russ himself had described his beloved Valomilks, which struck me, in the cold, carpeted glare of the Kansas City airport, as a suitable summation of the human condition: "They're dangerous," he said. "The filling gets all over the place. That's just how they're made."

A DEPRESSING BUT NECESSARY DIGRESSION

I now must make my own disturbing confession, which is that I went to take a leak in the airport bathroom and, while somewhat absently fondling myself *down there* (something that every red-blooded American male does, though perhaps not quite as often as I do), I felt a lump, or what I imagined to be a lump, and became convinced, almost at once, that *I* had cancer and that I would die.

With the benefit of hindsight, along with a physical exam

conducted by an actual doctor, I can happily diagnose this as a *hysterical episode*. But at the time, I was totally convinced. And thus, my feeling state—which was, as you have no doubt already observed, lurching from hyper to disconsolate—gave way to a sustained panic. I spent much of the next week gingerly palpating myself. Each time I felt the lump (which was every time, because the lump was, in fact, a necessary part of my male functioning, called the epididymis), dread would squirt through my chest cavity and my heart would start spazzing out. Then I would begin to get maudlin. I would consider my life and decide that it had been a terrible failure, a desperate plea for attention, a romantic wasteland, a creative mediocrity, and now it was over and what did I have to show for myself?

I realize that I am oversharing. I realize further that, should we ever meet in person, you might have justifiable reservations about shaking my hand. But the story of my trip would be incomplete without this disclosure, as it weighed so heavily upon me. And it's important to know this, too: the only time I forgot entirely about my impending death was when I lost myself in candy.

10

BOISE: GATEWAY TO . . . BOISE

I had never visited Idaho before, though I had some conception of the place as large and cold and mostly barren, a western cousin of the Dakotas. I knew, also, that it had a funny shape, a long, slim handle that stretched all the way to Canada. That was about it.

My flight had come in from Denver, where, on a scintillating two-hour layover, I guiltily consumed a McDonald's chicken sandwich, which tasted like cayenne pepper and industrial soap. By the time the pilot announced our initial descent into Boise, it was nearly eleven. I remember gazing down from my window seat. I expected to see the lights of the city laid out in neat yellow rows. There was nothing but a yawning black space cut into strips by the blue lights of the runways. The flight must have come in to Boise from the east. But all I could think was: *Where'd they put the city?*

As luck would have it, my visit coincided with a convention of the International Association of Arson Investigators. I felt a twinge of dread when I saw this announcement on the Holiday Inn marquee, because, as a twelve-year-old, out on the mean streets of south Palo Alto, I had nearly been arrested for arson. What had happened was this: my friend Brian Danforth and I had decided to explore a small, abandoned building along El Camino Real. This was totally normal twelve-year-old behavior, predicated on the belief that abandoned buildings contained piles of forgotten cash.

In this case, we did not find forgotten money. We found a little room in back with most of the walls busted out and lots of interesting trash on the ground, including an empty pack of Zig-Zags and part of a girlie magazine. It was the kind of place that twelve-year-old boys, in lieu of money, hope to find: covert and dilapidated, with the stink of sin all around. One or another of us lit a match, so as to see the girlie magazine in more detail, and the next thing we knew we were being ordered to freeze by a uniformed cop. I had never been spoken to by a cop.

There were two cops actually, beefy-armed and humorless, and they led us to their police cruiser and asked us to place our hands on the vehicle and spread our legs. The radios on their shoulders hummed and crackled and issued bursts of strangled words and numbers, which terrified us more than the cops themselves. (Were we going *there?*) The cop who found us patted me down and removed from my pocket a half-eaten Big Hunk. The bar still had my teeth marks. I found this a humiliating sight, especially in the context of a possible arrest scenario. I imagined having to check my belongings in prison. *(Hey boys, looks like we got us a really hard case! Look what he did to this here Big Hunk!)* The cop explained that he could place us under arrest, right then, for trespassing, as well as suspicion of arson, but that he was going to let us go if we promised to stay away from abandoned buildings. It must have occurred to him by then that we were not exactly towering criminal minds.

My point: I wasn't much in the mood for grabbing a nightcap in the bar, which was filled with men in glowering mustaches who could be heard muttering terms such as *solvent extraction* and *microtaggants*. I went to my room instead and palpated myself about 25 times and contemplated the poignancy of my untimely death. And when I got tired of this, I turned on the TV and watched the midterm election results. The Republicans were stomping the Democrats. Poor Walter Mondale, recruited to replace the last actual liberal in the Senate, the late Paul Wellstone, was addressing his supporters in some lousy hotel ballroom. He looked like a man brought out of storage and reinflated to not-quite life-size. What an embarrassment it was. The Bush tax cut had sopped the rich and wiped out the federal surplus. The economy was in the crapper. Dubya was doing everything in his power to hand the planet to Exxon. And America couldn't get enough of his abuse!

Two years earlier, I'd sat in front of another TV and watched him steal the presidency in broad daylight. Then a bunch of vicious airborne murderers had come along and scared the common sense out of everyone. In one morning, they'd managed to bestow upon this evangelical simpleton an air of presidential dignity. He saw his chance and bounced the rubble in Afghanistan and kept the bellows of war going (Iraq was next) and now the Democrats were too chickenhearted to oppose him. It was the poor who were going to pay, as they always do, and who gave a damn about them?

But then, who was I to bitch about all this? I hadn't even voted! I'd just flounced off on my candyland adventure without even bothering to consider my civic duty, and so, in some sense, I *deserved* the damage that Dubya was no doubt going to inflict on our country's already limited capacities for mercy, though, actually, none of this really mattered that much, because (lest we forget) I was *dying*. I snapped off the TV and listened to the muted rumble of the arson investigators in the bar across the breezeway and ate my way through a box of chocolate-covered pretzels and lay on my hotel bed in the dark with chocolate on my teeth, fuming like the good, useless liberal I am.

LADIES AND GENTLEMEN, THE IDAHO SPUD

So I woke up with a pretty severe electoral hangover. It called to mind the morning after the Reagan versus Mondale election of 1984. I was a freshman in college, appropriately bereaved, wandering down my dorm hall when I saw a large, bearish figure in shower sandals lumbering toward me. This was Seth Bergstein, the hall's resident hockey player. "We kicked your ass," Seth boomed. "Your guy got three points! Three lousy points!"

This was who led the country now. Seth Bergstein led the country.

My phone rang and Dave Wagers, the president of Idaho Candy Company, told me he was waiting in the parking lot out front. I went to the lobby and looked outside and saw a large white SUV with the license plate CANDMAN. *Please,* I said to myself, *don't let this guy be a Seth Bergstein.*

He was not. Let me go on record as stating that Dave Wagers is the coolest president of a candy company on earth. I say this not solely because he spent a day showing me around his factory, but because he did so in a way that suggested an authentic fascination with his chosen vocation. Dave's basic attitude was: *I make candy. It's pretty cool to make candy. Do you want some candy?* I don't fault guys like Russ Sifers or Marty Palmer for hamming it up a little. That's part of their job. But it was refreshing to meet a guy who seemed, frankly, pretty clueless when it came to self-promotion.

There were other reasons to like Dave Wagers. At 36, he was the youngest president I had encountered. He dressed in jeans and a sweatshirt. He looked a lot like Richie Brockleman, the eager, dorky PI who did his apprenticeship with Jim Rockford on the *Rockford Files* and whom I viewed as a role model through much of my adolescence. Dave had not heard of Richie Brockleman. "The one I get most of the time is Robert Kennedy," he told me. This was true. Dave had the same blue eyes and a strong, slightly overcrowded jaw. The problem is that Robert Kennedy was so terribly serious. Dave was just way more *chill* than Robert Kennedy.

So we got in his SUV and cruised toward downtown. There were construction projects on both sides of the road. These were big cookie-cutter homes, the sort that eventually compose developments with names like Splendid Oaks and White River. Boise was growing like crazy. When Dave was a kid, the city had a population of 50,000, twice that in the outlying area. Those numbers had quadrupled. This was the fundamental paradox of recent American migration patterns: people kept seeking a life away from the big city, in towns like Boise, thus turning towns like Boise into . . . big cities.

Boise, however, was not a big city in the coastal sense of that word. Aside from the grand old statehouse and a few half-hearted skyscrapers, the downtown was low-slung and relaxed. It was nestled in a mountainous valley on the western fringe of the Boise National Forest, which covered most of the state. Recently, high-tech companies such as Hewlett-Packard and Micron had opened factories in town, but agriculture was still the dominant industry. The state produced nearly a third of the country's potatoes.

Idaho Candy had been around since 1901, and in the same factory since 1909. "We're probably the only manufacturer still downtown," Dave said. We had pulled into a parking lot near the domed statehouse. He hopped out of his truck and made his way toward a loading dock and found a toehold in the cracked concrete and pulled himself onto the dock. I didn't quite understand at first. Then it struck me: this was how the president of Idaho Candy entered his factory.

I thought: *I can rally with this.*

"Here's where we keep the sugar," Dave said, wending his way through sacks the size of small hatchbacks. "The second biggest sugar factory in America is fifteen miles away and they deliver, which is kind of nice. We take the sugar up on this hydraulic lift, then it gets blown up a tube and onto the roof." I didn't quite get how one could *blow* sugar up onto a roof, but I didn't have time to ask Dave. He was eager to get up to the third floor, so he could check on what he called "the new machine," a 20-year-old starch mogul he had purchased from the

Henry Heide factory in New Jersey. The machine had been flown across the country and lowered through the roof of Dave's factory a week earlier. The mogul was crucial to any number of his products, but chiefly to the company's flagship bar, the Idaho Spud.

The third floor was a long, rectangular room lit by wide overhead skylights. Shafts of sun lit the maple floors and glinted off the steel machinery. It was like a shot out of Hitchcock—at once harsh and starkly beautiful. Dave kept getting offers to lease the space out as a loft, the most recent from a photographer who was awed by the quality of light in the room.

We arrived at a machine shaped like a deep pit barbeque, the whipper. Dave swung the lid open. The whipper was filled with an off-white liquid streaked in brown and speckled with air bubbles. "That's our *Spud*," Dave said, giving the word a hayseed inflection. Spud was basically a marshmallow filling composed of sugar, corn syrup, egg whites, and salt, and flavored with maple, vanilla, and dried cocoa (thus the brown streaks). Most marshmallows contain gelatin, to make them chewy. The Spud used a seaweed derivative called ager ager. At Dave's urging, I inspected a bucket of ager ager. It emanated a distinct and not pleasing odor. On the ground beneath the bucket was a pool of congealed agar agar, slick and translucent, with a rubbery consistency like cartilage.

Dave could see that I was in a state of moderate disgust.

"It's pretty wild stuff," he said. "They use it for petri dishes, growing cultures in labs. At the end of the day, there's always this weird crust in the whipper that we have to pull out. But what the agar agar does is gives the Spud a real resilience." He walked over to the mogul and removed one of the cured fillings. "Give it a try," Dave said. "Without the coating, you'll really be able to taste the maple."

I may have implied earlier that the Twin Bing was the strangest candy bar I saw on my sojourn. The Idaho Spud was far stranger. The filling was shaped like a Twinkie and surprisingly heavy. It had a sickly, grayish tint. I briefly considered telling Dave that I was allergic to products derived from seaweed. Or that I had a spastic colon. But the one thing you didn't do, in the presence of the president of a candy company, was refuse to sample product. What you did—to borrow a charming phrase from my creative writing students—was *sack it up*. I took a bite.

I will not pretend that I loved the Spud. (What I loved was the *idea* of the Spud.) But I was pleasantly surprised. There was indeed a delicate maple undertone to the piece, as well as a hint of cocoa. Most striking was the texture.

"It's a little like tofu," I said. "It has that same density."

"Right," Dave said. "A tofu marshmallow. You know, in the twenties and thirties the Spud was actually billed as the healthful candy bar, because of the agar agar. It's one of our most expensive ingredients. We pay nine dollars a pound for our agar agar."

Dave considered this fact gravely, before turning his attention to the mogul.

"What's going on, Greg?" he said.

Greg was his candy maker, a burly gentleman who wore his hairnet under a gimme cap that was caked in cornstarch. The overall effect was not unlike an Arab headdress.

"Something's wrong with the depositor," Greg said.

He pressed a button on the mogul's control panel and the great machine lurched into motion. An army of trays, each with 36 Spud molds, came trundling forward. The cured Spuds, rousted from their molds, thumped about in clouds of cornstarch. Greg had already pumped the Spud filling from the whipper into a large hopper suspended above the mogul. This liquid was fed into a series of nozzled valves, which were supposed to squirt the filling into the oncoming molds. They did so perfectly on the first set of molds. But with the second set, the valves squirted a half-second too early. The result of this premature, er, *depositation* was that only a portion of the filling made it into the mold. The rest spilled over the edge.

Dave and Greg peered at the depositor.

DAVE: Why would that be?
GREG: Timing chain?

DAVE: Doesn't make any sense.
GREG: You messed with the timing chain yesterday, right?
DAVE: Yeah, but I didn't take any links out.
GREG: Did you adjust a gear ratio or something? By mistake?
DAVE: Nope. (pause) Did you try turning it off and on?
GREG: Yeah, tried that already.

Greg turned off the machine and Dave stuck his head pretty much inside the depositor. Then he stepped back and took hold of something—I'll assume it was the timing chain—and told Greg to turn on the mogul. As the second set of molds came forward, Dave gave the chain a brisk jerk. The Spuds came out perfect. This was not a tenable situation, though. You couldn't have the president jerking at the mogul all day.

During all this activity, an elderly gentleman in a dark blazer and necktie had appeared at the top of the stairs. He stood, patiently waiting for Dave to notice him.

"Machine broke?" he said, after a time.

Dave turned and nodded. He introduced his father—"The guy who got me into all this"—and went back to inspecting the mogul with Greg.

John Wagers was a soft-spoken, solidly built man in the Jack Kemp mold. His official title was Chairman of the Board. Although he was supposed to be retired, he conceded, a bit sheepishly, that he still came out to the factory most days, to see what his youngest son was up to.

For most of his life, John Wagers had been an accountant. In 1982, he sold his practice and semiretired. He was, in his own words, "just puttering around" when a friend approached him about the prospect of buying Idaho Candy. (The purchase price included a snack distribution business, as well.) Three weeks later John, who knew nothing about the candy industry, was the owner.

In a sense, he was carrying on a company tradition. The founder, T. O. Smith, had moved to Boise in 1900 not to make candy, but to build a hotel. Once the hotel was finished he, too, found himself at loose ends. A former confectioner, he started making candy out of his garage and selling it door-to-door.

John described Smith as "a real visionary in the candy world" who invented more than 100 different candies in his lifetime. The Spud came along in 1926. "Would you like to see some of the molds Smith used?" John said. He led me to a shelf tucked away in the far corner of the room and, with a tremendous delicacy, as if handling Picasso's paintbrushes, removed one rack of molds after another. They were lovely: rows of scalloped shells, pyramids, gumdrops. "This one's my favorite," John said. "Elephants. Will you look at that? Elephants."

John had been charged with overseeing the production of

a new set of molds for the Spuds and another candy bar, the Old Faithful. Dave had gotten the idea of making new molds after running into his old shop teacher from junior high. He was paying a bunch of thirteen-year-old burnouts, in other words, to make his new molds. This struck me as something Mars would not do.

Idaho Candy produced a third bar called the Cherry Cocktail, which looked quite similar to the Twin Bing. The difference, John explained, was that he and Dave used a *real* chocolate coating, and put *real* cherries inside. This was done by hand. He went into great and loving detail about the use of inverted sugar in the fondant, because this ingredient was what allowed the fondant to liquefy after the chocolate coating had been applied. "What you want, you see, is a filling that's juicy and delicious," John said.

Behind us, the mogul chugged to life.

"Looks like you fixed it," John called over to his son.

Dave shrugged. "We had to move the timing chain one link. My lucky day."

"It's not luck," John said.

"Right now it's luck, Dad."

"I was telling this young man about the new molds," John said.

It was funny to watch the old fellow, this former accountant with dabs of cornstarch on the cuffs of his fancy blazer. He was still puttering around, in a sense. But his props were much more interesting now. He pulled his son aside to discuss a private matter. Greg and the rest of the cook crew went back to their routine, sliding buckets across the floor, wheeling racks of wet Spuds through the slender shafts of sunlight.

I was the only one, therefore, to see what happened next, which was that the grayish brown liquid Spud began gurgling over the sides of the depositor. My initial thought was: *How interesting! The filling is bubbling over! I wonder how this is supposed to work?* It was when the liquid Spud starting to drip down onto the control panel that I realized I was witnessing a major malfunction.

"I think," I said, "should that be . . ." Thick sheets of the gluey stuff had, by now, enveloped the nozzles and hoses below. I thought, absurdly, of Dr. Seuss: a world awash in Oobleck. "There seems to be a problem—"

Greg looked up and shouted something unintelligible and Dave and his father wheeled around and then both Dave and Greg were leaping for the big red button on the control panel. The machine ground to a halt. For a few moments, the only sound was the soft glottal slurp of liquid Spud dripping onto and off of steel fixtures.

"Shit," Dave said thoughtfully.

I immediately began apologizing. I felt I had caused this disaster. My presence had been a distraction, I had failed to say something sooner.

Dave shook his head. "This happened before."

"Third time this week," Greg said. "Anyway, you should have seen the old mogul. I had that thing held together with Band-Aids and duct tape."

This was supposed to be a disaster, a minor one anyway. But no one was treating it as a disaster. We were all just staring at the mogul, watching the strings of Spud rill down the bright metal. It was quite beautiful, actually, the sort of tableau one might expect to find in an East Village art gallery, a testament to the enduring fallibility of technology. Machines depended on men. They could still break down in the loveliest of ways. What struck me as most enchanting was the sense of executive engagement in the manufacturing process. The president of Idaho Candy wasn't tucked away in some swank office reviewing marketing studies while some underpaid drone did the dirty work. He was elbow deep in Spud, just as T. O. Smith would have been a century before. And more than this, he *wanted* to be elbow deep in Spud, spattered in cornstarch, his fingertips perfumed with the strange sea scent of ager ager. This is what a candymaker did! He worked with ingredients, dove into the sweet muck of invention, jerked the necessary timing chains. The fact that something had gone wrong wasn't a cause for panic or despondence, but, in some manner, for celebration. What joy would there be in a world without adversity? I even got Dave and his dad to pose for a picture in front of the spill. Sure. What the heck? They didn't mind.

HUCKLEBERRY, HOUNDED

Later, Dave led me down to the second floor. Idaho Candy was a general merchandising house, much like Palmer Candy, though the organizational scheme of the factory was way more free-form. The central visual component of the second floor, for instance, was a pair of long white cooling tables scattered with several thousand bright green . . . somethings. A thick effluvium of vanilla wafted about.

Dave picked up a handful and popped them into his mouth.

"These are practically my favorite things we make," he said. "Burnt peanuts."

Actually, they were roasted peanuts in a sugar and vanilla coating, and they were, as billed, mindblowingly delicious.

"Right?" Dave said. He took another handful.

"How do you get them to look like this?"

The coating was composed of dozens of tiny little beads.

"That's a pebbling effect," Dave said. "We add salt when they go in the pan and the sugar gathers around the salt granules."

In the back of the room, a worker was making a batch of red peanuts, ladling a syrup that looked like movie blood into a roaring panning machine. The two colors would later be combined to make a Christmas mix. The room smelled like a Chinese restaurant, owing to the warm exhaust pumping out of the peanut roaster.

What Dave really wanted to show me, though, was a new product called the Huckleberry Imperial. I was familiar, if vaguely, with Huckleberry Hound. But I was not aware that there was such a thing as an actual huckleberry. There was. It was the state fruit of Idaho, a small, fragrant purple berry. The Huckleberry Imperial was a small purple hard candy, something like a cinnamon red hot. Dave ransacked the various shelves and boxes in the panning department, and ran downstairs to check one other place. Alas, he was unable to find a Huckleberry Imperial. In the end, I had to settle for a somewhat aged pillow candy, which still managed to convey a sense of the huckleberry gestalt: similar to a boysenberry, but fruitier, more intense. There were other products Dave wanted me to try, including the storied Chicken Bone, a crunchy peanut-butter stick of the Chick-o-Stick genus, along with a piquant horehound hard candy based on the tea, and something called Peco Brittle, which involved large coconut shavings. (I shan't dwell.) But the piece that made Dave get all misty-eyed was his Owyhee Butter Toffee. He'd done some major work with this toffee, upgrading the quality of the piece and designing a new box. We tromped to the front of the building, where a half dozen women were dipping pieces of the toffee in a thin marshmallow paste and rolling them in crushed almonds.

Let me say this about Owyhee Butter Toffee: if you are one of those people who views butter as the high point of western culinary achievement, as I do, track down some of this stuff. It was like sucking on a sugar cube sautéed in butter, only much much smoother. (The piece was 17 percent butter; my initial estimate had been 87 percent.) Dave also insisted I try one of his new creations: a cashew brittle covered in dark chocolate. This was basically the Platonic ideal of a Heath bar. Each bite delivered a rich, slightly bitter surge of cocoa, sweetened by the toffee, and slowly relented to a mellow cashew afterburn. So Dave wasn't just the guy who fixed the machines. He had also caught the bug of invention. And he was good. He had a knack for blending flavors and textures. He understood—like any freak alchemist—that a truly special piece of candy should surprise and enthrall the mouth, should be both intuitive and revolutionary. (Side note: I later had to physically restrain myself from stealing a box of the cashew brittle.)

The second floor was crowded with older equipment: brass drop molds, a batch roller that dated back to World War I, a row of fearsome-looking antique candy cutters. Dave seemed endlessly fascinated by this stuff, and I couldn't really blame him. It is one of the few privileges of modernity to regard the innovations of the recent past as quaint, rather than barbaric. But they are more than quaint. They are reminders of the era when men and machines worked in concert to produce objects, before technology became mysterious and abstract, a series of ones and zeros floating above us in the stratosphere, or hidden away in circuit boards and servers. And Dave, bless his Luddite heart, had no great ambitions to modernize the factory. His cooling system for hard candies, for example, was composed of air hoses attached to the underside of a slender steel canopy. It looked like someone had laid out the Tin Man from *The Wizard of Oz*.

Dave insisted I try another new product, the Spud Bite. I had feared this moment would come eventually. A finished Spud includes not just the queer discolored tofu-marshmallow, but a coating of chocolate rolled in . . . coconut. The Bite tasted a lot better than I thought it would, though. And I'm not just saying that in the hopes that Dave will send me a free box of Owyhee Butter Toffee, though obviously, I would not turn away such generosity. No, I liked the Spud Bite. The coconut was of the medium-dry variety, meaning that it didn't have that creepy cuticle texture. It was, instead, pleasantly crunchy. The bite contained 40 percent more chocolate than its full-size cousin (Dave had done the math) and this helped sharpen up the mellow maple flavor of the filling. There was, I am further pleased to report, no seaweed aftertaste.

Down in the dim basement, a gruff gentleman named Gary was keeping watch over the company's enrober. The Spud fillings were set onto a conveyor belt and sent chugging into a familiar curtain of chocolate, after which they passed under a machine called a coconut depositor—second only to the *nut applicator* in my patheon of favorite freak appliances—which snowed flakes onto the still-wet chocolate.

"That's probably the only coconut depositor in operation in the entire United States of America," Gary said. "I've been with Idaho for 34 years, and it came in just before I got here. Up till then the Spuds used to come off the back end and drop into a big slab of coconut and the girls would roll them around in there and put them into the cooling tunnel."

Back in the old days, Dave said, the Spud had looked quite different. It was composed of two centers stuck together with milk chocolate, so as to resemble an actual potato, rather than half a potato. Old-timers still occasionally asked Dave when he was going to start making Spud bars the right way again.

Gary walked to the end of the line and came back with a candy bar in a red, white, and blue wrapper. "Has he tried one of these yet?"

"This is our Old Faithful," Dave said.

I'd done a good deal of fantasizing about what the Old

Faithful might entail. The Spud, after all, was clearly shaped like a potato (or a half potato) and there was even some indication, based on the wrapper, that the coconut flakes on the outside were an attempt to simulate the eyes of a potato. So I had taken to envisioning the Old Faithful as a geyser of chocolate, exploding forth with wavelets of caramel and crisped rice. This was positively absurd, but it is how my mind operates.

The Old Faithful was not a geyser. It was more like a small brick. I took a bite of the bar and inspected the cross section: a strip of marshmallow, topped by a thick band of milk chocolate, shot through with whole roasted peanuts. The arbitrary distribution of these peanuts gave the bar a lumpy, roguish look.

"We're working on a new mold for this one," Dave said.

"Yeah," I said. "I was thinking you might want to play off the geyser angle a little more, give the bar some upward motion. Like a geyser."

Gary had heard enough from me. He tipped his cap and turned to his next task, while Dave and I moved on to the wrapping section. The Foreigner tune that had been issuing from the radio in the enrobing area gave way to the tinkling treacle of the Alan Parsons Project.

"Hey, take a look at this," Dave said. He gestured to a fifties-era box of Spuds whose fading legend read, A 60 CENT VALUE WITH 6 BARS! Dave flipped the box over. On the back was a set of *international recipes*: Idaho Spud Mousse in a Mold

(France), Neapolitan Spud Cake (Italy), Chocolate Cream Spud Pie (Bavaria), and, of course, Idaho Spud Fondue (Switzerland).

"That's the one we like," Dave said.

"Seriously?" I said.

"Oh yeah. It's really easy. You just melt six Spuds in a fondue pot. We made it last week for a dinner party."

I didn't know quite what to say. Dave hadn't struck me as a fondue sort of guy. I saw him more in the bean dip milieu.

We went upstairs to Dave's unofficial office. It had a desk with a gallon bottle of vanilla on it, but no chair. In one corner of the room was a foot-thick steel door embossed with gold leaf. This was the old company safe, which was being used as a closet.

Dave seemed totally at ease in his role as president, but he assured me it was not what he'd envisioned when he graduated from the University of Idaho with a degree in accounting. Instead, he'd gone to work for EDS, Ross Perot's old company. He found himself, at age 25, zooming up the corporate ladder. The problem was that he didn't really want to be. So he quit. It was at this juncture that his father urged him (*urged* is probably too gentle a word) to return to Boise to run the company.

"I showed up for my first day of work in a suit and the employees were like, 'What the hell is this?' " Dave said. "There was this one woman, Violet Brewer was her name. She'd worked for Idaho Candy for 82 years. She knew everything there was to know about the factory. Her friend told me she took one look at me and said, 'Well, who's going to fix the machines?' "

Dave's cell phone rang. It was Greg from upstairs. The mogul was broken again. He went upstairs to inspect the situation. When he came back down, an elderly blond woman in a garish blue windbreaker was waiting for him. Dave was wearing a hairnet and there were splotches of cornstarch all over his jeans. The woman looked at him nervously. "Are you really the owner?"

"What was that about?" I asked, when she took her leave.

"She wants to sell some of our old stuff on e-Bay," Dave said, "the old wooden candy trays and stuff. I suppose we could describe them as collector's items. They do have the residue of candy made a century ago." He paused. "That's what I like about this job—the breadth of it. I used to be an accountant, costing out billion-dollar contracts. Now I have to handle everything. Marketing, production, distribution, sales. I don't have some big staff to test-market this or that. When I want to try something new, I go ask my friends what they think. It's very seat-of-the-pants. I was drinking beer one night with a friend and we were like, 'Hey, what can we do?' We came up with chocolate-covered potato chips." (I later bought a bag of these at this little Idaho tourist shop down the street. The combination of fried starch and chocolate was unstoppable, the snap of the chips pleasingly muted by the thin coat of chocolate.)

Dave had left the coat-and-tie aspect of accounting behind, but he remained fascinated by the internal minutiae of his business. He showed me a pair of company audits from the twenties, handsome, leather-bound volumes, which he handled with elaborate care. The itemizations included a steel starch bucker ($1,100), a vacuum kettle ($1,500), and the very trays Dave was now considering selling on e-Bay (35 cents apiece). He gingerly unfolded an architectural drawing of the plant from 1925 and was about to compare this factory layout to his current setup, when he bolted upright. "Shoot," he said. "I'm late for a parent/teacher conference."

AMERICAN LUNCH

Before he dashed off, Dave recommended a few lunch options, including a place called the Beanery, and a Basque restaurant, whose menu included a great deal of lamb. It turned out that the Basque were some of the region's earliest European settlers. They'd come in the 1890s to make their fortune as sheepherders. I know this because I stopped in at the chamber of commerce and read a bunch of pamphlets. I was also intrigued to learn a little more about Idaho's leading exports. Potatoes get most of the play, but I am here to tell you that the state produces more than three-quarters of the nation's trout, and 93 percent of its Austrian winter peas.

It was a gorgeous late autumn day, around 60 degrees; I could see why the Basque had set down roots. Boise had a spiffy new downtown plaza, with sidewalks designed to look aged and a sleek convention center. I couldn't help but notice that there was a steady stream of people passing into and out of this convention center, so I went over to investigate. The lobby was festooned with balloons. A cheerful young woman in a bright red polo shirt walked up to me. "Welcome to Food Expo 2002!" she said. "Who are you here representing?"

I paused for a moment. I could see a bright strip of light leaking from beneath the doors to the main hall. Every few seconds someone emerged from the bustle within and a bouquet of bacon and pizza dough came wafting thickly forth. I was, it dawned on me, quite hungry. I was also, for once in my life, neatly dressed. The girl in the red shirt stood before me, her face cast in the polite rictus of the service industry.

"Idaho Candy Company," I said.

"Well, welcome!" She thrust a promotional gift bag into my hand. "You'll find all your order forms in here."

"Excellent," I said.

I walked briskly toward the main hall. As I was about to hit the door, I heard someone call out behind me. "Sir! Sir!"

I turned.

My greeter motioned urgently at her lapel. "Don't forget your name tag!"

What can I tell you about Food Expo 2002? It was the most potent dose of American culinary culture I had ever experienced. Everywhere I looked a salesperson was begging me to taste something designed to kill me: cheesecake, chicken wings, guacamole, French fries, cheese sticks, pork dumplings, popcorn shrimp, pudding cups, kielbasa, corndogs, chili burgers, deviled eggs, brownies, Popsicles, waffle cones brimming with ice cream and freshly zapped hot fudge.

The Expo was aimed at restaurants and clubs, the great, greasy grazing yards of the lonely American nomad—which was me. And how tenderly the staffers worked at their enticements! With microwaves and Crock-Pots, they prepared dainty cups of chowder and pizza pockets; they heaped plates with chop suey and twirled shiny morsels of stew on colored toothpicks, their ardent hopeless faces sweating a little under the heat lamps. And all this preparation accompanied by a machine-gun patter of quality ingredients and easy prep and no mess and low stress. *These guys, you just bang em out. Put em on a plate with some ranch dressing, tartar, whatever you please. That's right, flash frozen. It's an exclusive process. The Swedes came up with it. Locks in the natural flavor enzymes. Now, I'm not going to run down the other guys, but you check the ingredients in their breading, you see what they put in there. I'm just proud to be able to offer this product. Look at that texture. Taste that. How does that taste? Be honest. Is that not the finest fish stick on God's green earth?*

This was the giant, leering craw of the corporate food industry, which was all about convenience, the quick profits of the prefab patty, the potato skin, the suet-shimmering flimflammery of our ravenous fat merchants. Dave's operation looked positively organic by comparison.

I spent half an hour drifting from one booth to the next, listening, nodding, opening my mouth, chewing, before I experienced a sensation so alien to me as to seem perverse: *the desire for a vegetable*. The closest I'd come so far, if you don't count kale—which I don't—was a grilled artichoke heart. (It will go without saying that I had not encountered a single Austrian winter pea.)

I consulted my program, to no avail. At last, I spotted a flash of greenery along the far wall and hurried over. A dispirited blond woman seemed to be breaking down the booth, which included a pile of carrots and bell peppers.

"What are you selling?" I said.

"Frozen vegetables," she muttered.

"They look great," I said. "Great-looking vegetables."

"Those are props," she said.

"Right."

"The product is a diced, frozen vegetable medley. But I'm

closed for the day." She must have felt like a Hare Krishna at a tent revival.

"I understand completely," I said. "But I'd love a pepper, if you can spare it."

She looked at me. "A pepper?"

"Yeah. One of those peppers."

"Those are props," she said again. "They're shellacked."

HOW WILL THE SPUD SURVIVE?

When I got back to the factory Dave was poring over the old ledgers. He'd found some sales figures. "We made a profit of $50,000 in 1918. Then, the next year, we had revenues of $255,000, which is, like, $25 million today. We were probably one of the top 20 candy companies in the country at that point. We provided all the candy for the state of Idaho and beyond. I look at these numbers and just drool."

Dave clearly had a soft spot for history. He also had a sense of perspective, though. He knew what came next: the lean years of the Depression, the rise of the national giants, then, the darkest hour—a spectacularly misguided effort, during the sixties, to take the Spud bar national. Dave harbored no such fantasies. He knew that the Spud was mostly a novelty product, something folks bought at the airport and brought home as a souvenir. He made 3 million Spuds per year, 120,000 Cherry

Cocktails, and 60,000 Old Faithfuls. Mars made that many Snickers bars in an *afternoon*. His hopes for the growth of the manufacturing side were modest, a few percent a year, if possible.

Ironically, he said, it was the distribution side of the business—a venture he dismissed as "just moving boxes from here to there"—that had thrived, more than tripling in size over the past 20 years. Dave had more than 9,000 items in his warehouse, which he sold to some 800 different supermarkets and convenience stores. He was intimately familiar with the realpolitik of modern retail.

"There's an unbelievable amount of money that flows into the back of the chains," he said. And not just in slotting fees. Virtually every time a company places a product in a store, they pay in some form. A presell, which is two weeks of free product. Or a discount on price. Idaho Candy couldn't afford any of this, so they tended to get lost. "The big guys say, 'I'm sorry, we're paying $20,000 per store and we don't want any of that other bullshit in there.' When I deal with them as a manufacturer, they're friendly enough. But in the store, it's brutal."

There was little Dave could do to increase demand for the Spud, let alone a bar like the Old Faithful. He practiced some guerilla marketing, giving Spuds to the cheerleaders at Boise State games to throw out to the crowd, that kind of stuff. He was also considering individually wrapping Spud Bites and doing more specialty products.

I myself had been thinking about a possible new bar on my way back from lunch, the Huckleberry Hound: a huckleberry-flavored nougat covered in bittersweet chocolate. I could see the soft purple of the nougat framed by dark chocolate, and I could taste it as well, the sweet fruity fluff tempered by coffee tones. I realized there might be some hassle regarding the name, but Hanna-Barbera (or whoever owned the copyright) could eventually be prevailed upon. This was synergy, after all. Cross promotion.

Dave's response was, well, muted. "I do want to do more with the huckleberry," he said, cautiously. "But I was thinking more like a Huckleberry Cocktail."

It was getting on toward four. Dave offered to drive me to the airport. We could pay a visit to the distribution warehouse on the way. And, of course, he wanted to give me a few candy bars for the road, so we took one last swing through the factory. Before we could get too far, a young woman called over to Dave in a distinct tone of anguish. She pointed to an older woman, who was cradling her left hand in her right.

"What happened here?" Dave said.

"The glue gun," the young woman said.

The older woman held out her hand. A nasty pink welt ran half the length of her thumb. Dave winced and ran off to get the first aid kit and when he came back he said, "You need to run that under some cold water and put some disinfectant on and then put a bandage on it. Take the disinfectant home if you need to. Change the bandage frequently. And remember that glue gun is *really* hot."

Both women nodded. They appeared to have picked up on this already.

We left the factory via the loading dock and headed toward his warehouse. The sun had flattened out and turned the foothills around Boise a soft gold. The gentle, rolling terrain reminded me of northern California, without the oak trees. For more than a century, sheep had wandered these valleys, conducting their business in peace. Now a rash of fancy homes was creeping up the hillsides. If you listened carefully you could hear the hammers pounding away like cap guns.

Dave looked pretty beat. He'd been working about 100 hours per week to get the new mogul up and running. A regular week, he assured me, was half that. "My dad used to work 70 a week. My brothers still do. That's just too much for me. My wife, she only works three days a week. We're not going to earn a ton of money. It's just not our priority in life."

His wife was a dentist.

We came to a red light and the car beside us tooted its horn. Dave looked over and waved.

"Who's that?"

"Don't know. They probably just saw the license plate. People in town sort of know me as the Candyman."

We pulled up to the warehouse, which was basically a convenience store on the scale of an airport hangar. To me, an admitted fat junkie, this was a mesmerizing setting, and I spent many minutes traipsing the endless rows of chips and Skittles and Slim Jims. Dave seemed restless. The truth was, he told me, he sometimes fantasized about selling off his great big snack palace. This was surely the wrong thing to do, in a business sense. But the place bored him silly. What he really wanted to show me was the new box he'd designed for Owyhee Butter Toffee.

And so, after I'd finished ogling all the various munchies (and not, despite severe kleptomaniacal pangs, stealing any of them) he led me back to his office and set the box on a thick layer of invoices and order forms.

"What do you think?" he asked me.

I assured him the box was gorgeous. And it was. There was a photograph of the Idaho Candy Company taken in the thirties, showing a line of black cars and men in waistcoats posing out front. This was set against a matte background with gold trim. Beside the photograph was a brief history of the toffee recorded in elegant script.

He asked me a few pointed questions, about color and composition. He wanted to make sure I wasn't patronizing him. Finally, he seemed satisfied and set the box down between us.

The more I talked with Dave, the more I was struck by his

similarity to Marty Palmer. Both men had forsaken a high-powered career and returned home to take over a family business. Both were former athletes (Dave had been a state-ranked tennis player) who had settled into family life and become civic leaders. When I mentioned this to Dave, he shook his head. "I'm not as hard a pusher as Marty," he said.

This is what I probably liked most about Dave Wagers, in the end. He retained a necessary fascination with the teleology of capitalism, which is to maximize profit. But he could also see that there was a spiritual price to be paid for all that striving. Roiling within him was a messier, less-profitable impulse—the wish to create.

11

THE PAST IS JUST AHEAD

I spent my entire youth eating the candy bars produced by the Annabelle Candy Company. I didn't know this at the time. I wasn't, as they say, an *informed consumer*. But the record stands: Hadn't the cop who nearly cuffed me for arson found on my person a half-eaten Big Hunk? Hadn't my older brother Dave once promised to give me an Abba-Zaba if I agreed to search the graveyard next to Terman Junior High for his Estes rocket? (And hadn't he subsequently reneged, claiming that an oral agreement did not constitute, as such, a binding contract?) Hadn't my father, the estimable Richard, once thrown a frozen Rocky Road across the room during a moment of paternal frustration. Or was that a U-no bar?

No matter. My point is that Annabelle candy bars were a touchstone of my youth. I knew the names and wrappers and tastes and textures by heart. Then, as happens in the modern candy game, they disappeared entirely from my life, once I left California. I spent a good many hours trying to explain the Big Hunk to friends from the East Coast.

Vanilla taffy? Vanilla taffy and peanuts? Sounds gross.

No, no. It's delicious. Really.

The problem was that I hadn't actually eaten a Big Hunk since I was fourteen.

So it was with a certain Homeric sense of closure that I strolled into Annabelle headquarters, located on the aptly named Industrial Boulevard in the gritty East Bay burg of Hayward. I was met, almost immediately, by Susan Karl, the president of Annabelle. A short, dark-haired woman in a blue blazer and slacks, she looked, if I may be candid, very much like my own mother (though, for the record, my mother has never worn red, square-framed glasses). The physical similarity was no doubt accentuated by Karl's demeanor, which I would describe as both highly competent and pleasantly neurotic.

"Okay," she said, ushering me into her office, "so you're working on something. What? A book? I'd like a copy of whatever you're going to write. And I'd prefer if you don't make me sound like an idiot." It was clear to me—and would become only more so—that making Susan Karl sound like an idiot would take some doing.

The company, she noted, was founded by her grandfather, Sam Altshuler, who immigrated from Russia in 1917, settled in San Francisco, and started making the Rocky Road in his kitchen. He sold the confection from a pushcart on Market Street. The business, which he named after his only child, failed several times. This did little to deter Altshuler. Above Karl's desk was a photo of the groundbreaking of the Hayward factory, taken in 1965. "The little girl is me," she said. "I was sick from school that day, so I got to come. Isn't that cool?"

Karl's memories of her grandfather were vivid. "He doted on me. I could do no wrong in his eyes. He lived with us for quite a while and what I remember is that he always smelled like chocolate and there was marshmallow all over his shoes every day. My friends thought that was so cool, but to me it was just, like, normal."

When Altshuler passed away, in 1971, his daughter, Annabelle, took over. Karl's brother took the helm some years later. Karl herself had little to do with the business. She moved to Los Angeles with her husband and became a prosecutor in the district attorney's office. After a decade, she was appointed as a judge in Malibu. "With the robe and the whole thing," she said. "I job-shared with a partner. We both had little kids, so part-time was perfect. I did civil and criminal, and I did have to put people in the slammer. Here's my best story. Do you want to hear my best story? You know Jim Belushi? Well, he had a speeding ticket and he went to trial before me. He was adorable. So funny! It was all I could do to keep from losing it during the trial. I had to sit there like this." Karl stared down at her desk with an expression of grim determination.

Five years ago, she and her husband decided to move back to the Bay Area. They were tired of L.A. No one read there. So Karl decided to take over the family business, a decision that made her brother and mother ecstatic. "We're profitable most years," Karl told me. "We have a very loyal following. If you grew up in this part of the country, you've heard of us. The only people who've never heard of us are on the East Coast. But even there we're making some headway. Take a look at this!"

She directed my attention to a copy of the *New York Times Magazine*. One of the articles was about Dylan Lauren's hip new Manhattan candy shop. The accompanying photo featured a selection of offbeat candy products and there, smack in the middle, were the Big Hunk and Look!

In fact, Annabelle products—on the basis of sheer quirkiness—made frequent appearances in the zeitgeist. A memorable episode of *Seinfeld* showed George Costanza at his desk. He opened the top drawer and there, pictured for a long moment, was a Big Hunk. (The irony, not lost on Karl, is that Big Hunk was not, at that time, even sold in New York, where the show was set.) Abba-Zabas played a major role in the film *Half Baked,* a Dave Chappelle vehicle that had become a minor cult classic amongst pothead teenagers. Karl still got people approaching her booth at trade shows, catching sight of the Abba-Zabas, and saying, "Hey, *Half Baked!*" This was just fine with her. She considered it free advertising.

Karl led me into the factory and up a set of stairs that allowed us a vista of the entire operation. It was a behemoth, 60,000 square feet in all, a jumble of catwalks and platforms and kettles and pipes and pumps, with dozens of workers in hard hats zipping to and fro across the wet concrete floor. From a distance it looked like industrial chaos, the sort of place Charlie Chaplin would have had a field day with.

Karl moved briskly through the machinery, bent slightly forward at the waist, like a general inspecting her troops. She was wearing a jaunty yellow hard hat. "Okay, first thing, you can't take any pictures of the area where we make Rocky Roads because the process is proprietary. Okay? My mother made me promise that I wouldn't let anyone take pictures so, I'm sorry, I have to abide by her word. She's still the boss, because she still owns a majority of the company, and besides, she's my mother."

"Okay," I said.

This caveat might lead one to expect that the production of the Rocky Road was ultramodern. It was not. In fact, the process was little changed from the days of Grandpa Altshuler. One whole corner of the factory was devoted to a quartet of metal tables about 70 feet long and 4 feet across. It was here that the marshmallow was laid out to cool overnight, given an initial layer of chocolate and crushed cashews, and cut into manageable squares. Further down the line, a worker was peeling the wax paper off the squares (they had the appearance of chocolate floor tiles) and feeding them into a device that cut them into strips. A device nicknamed the "octopus" separated each of the strips and fed them onto their own miniconveyor belt. Further down the line they would be cut into bar-size pieces and enrobed again, then cooled and wrapped.

The production of the Big Hunk began with peanuts, which were fried in oil, then hustled along a conveyor belt. "This woman is our inspector," Karl noted. "She does nothing but throw out any peanuts that don't look right. Like a peanut that's black or something. We get very few complaints."

In the center of the factory was a cooking area composed of no fewer than thirteen kettles. It now became clear to me why I'd been required to wear a hard hat—because some of these kettles were being raised into the air.

"This is where we actually cook our Big Hunk," Karl said.

"Smells like marshmallow," I said.

"No," she said brusquely. "The Big Hunk has nothing to do

with marshmallow." The very notion seemed to cause her physical discomfort. "It's a vanilla nougat with—"

"I thought it was taffy," I said.

"*Nougat,*" Karl said. "A vanilla *nougat* with peanuts."

"Isn't nougat supposed to be sort of fluffy?" I said.

Karl stared at me. "Well, alright, I guess it's a chewy nougat." She pointed to a huge kettle, which was being hoisted pretty much *over my head* and toward an even huger steel hopper. A worker in a brown apron stood on a raised platform. A sort of ballet ensued, in which the worker grabbed the kettle and angled its contents—a sticky white syrup now pebbled with peanuts—into the hopper. The liquid nougat then squirted through a spigot at the bottom of the hopper into a six-foot-long bread pan.

"What we do," Karl said, hurrying past the platform, "is we put the pans into these ovens here and cook the nougat. Then, once they've gotten to the right consistency, we take out the pans and what we've got is a loaf. The nougat is pretty hard to get out, so these guys have to slam the pans. You can hear it all over the building."

The loaves were then fed, two at a time, into a truly fearsome cutting machine called a Phizer, which sliced each loaf into slender bars. This process accounted for the unique look of the Big Hunk, which featured a cross section of browned peanuts floating in the white *nougat*. Karl picked up one of the bars from the assembly line. It drooped onto her fist. "The Big Hunk is the best when it's warm and soft like this," she said. "What we recommend is for people to pop them into the microwave for a few seconds. It's right on the back of the package."

REMEMBER THIS NAME: BANANA-ZABA

To see how the U-no bars were made, we took a trip to a place called the chocolate platform, a small, raised area that (as one might expect) was liberally decorated with chocolate. Indeed, it looked liked the scene of a particularly grisly chocolate homicide. The stuff was everywhere: dripping from the pipes, spattered on buckets and boxes, congealed into dark reddish pools on the floor. "Oh, this is terrible!" Karl said. "What a mess. This is the reason we don't usually show this area to anybody. You should know we're getting new machinery."

The filling for the U-no bars was basically milk chocolate whipped full of air and finely ground almonds. Karl showed me the machine that did this whipping; it was equipped with 20 blades, none of which I could actually see because they were moving way too fast. The resulting substance, which I am reluctant to categorize as either liquid or solid, was then piped downstairs to a machine called an extruder. I had heard a fair amount about the extruder in my candy travels and had envisioned something like a giant pastry funnel squeezed by means of a hydraulic pump or, perhaps, costumed dwarfs. The Annabelle extruder was a bit of a letdown, in that:

1. It was a large metal box; and
2. The exact mechanism of extrusion was concealed within this large metal box.

All I could see (and this only by squatting down and craning my neck) was the pale brown filling emerging from *somewhere* in the form of slender bars. Despite the pleasant aroma, the visual image was somewhat disconcerting, and I did not linger.

The bars were cooled, enrobed in a darker chocolate, then cooled again. I spent a minute or so hinting to Karl that I really wanted to try a U-no bar fresh off the line. She assured me that she would grab me some samples later. "They're really good frozen," she said. "They taste like mousse." But I was intrigued by the prospect of the ground almonds and intoxicated by the smell of the enrober and so I waited until Karl had turned to speak to her factory manager, Carlos, then grabbed a U-no bar that was lying on a rejects cart. I had about 30 seconds to eat the bar and did so, in three bites. (As a result of this decision I spent the rest of the day revisiting the U-no bar, in the form of flavored burps, a not-altogether-unpleasant arrangement.)

My feelings about the U-no were conflicted. On the one hand, I could see what Karl was talking about with her mousse comment. The bar did have pillowy texture. The ground almonds, while not really detectable on the tongue, lent the chocolate a rich, nutty undertone. The problem resided with what I'll call the fat quotient. Mousse, after all, tastes good because it's full of cocoa butter, and the mouth recognizes this at once. The U-no, by contrast, contained a good deal of air, and the result was an ineradicable sense of partial vacancy, of subterfuge—like eating a rice cake. I did not mention this to Karl, of course. I merely gulped down the bar and hoped that the line workers who had witnessed my act of thievery wouldn't rat me out.

I was most interested in seeing the Abba-Zaba being made. For those who have never had the good fortune of tasting an Abba-Zaba, it is easily distinguished as the only candy bar (that I know of) which contains peanut butter *inside* taffy. Indeed, the great joy of eating an Abba-Zaba resides in the peculiar oral aspects of combining these two candy genres, generally thought to be disparate. The American palette is accustomed, by this time, to chocolate and peanut butter. We think nothing of the combination, in part because both substances melt at about the same temperature. That is, they make the fateful transformation from solid to liquid contemporaneously. Not so with the Abba-Zaba. Taffy may soften, after all, but it remains resilient, essentially solid, in the gnashed heat of the mouth. The peanut butter, by contrast, yields almost immediately and begins a delicious process of seepage, so that you are left, in effect, with an organically rendered peanut butter taffy. (The same process abides with the Charleston Chew: the warmth of the tongue, along with the motion of the teeth, softens the taffy and infuses it with the melted chocolate coating.)

The Abba-Zaba was not in production, but Karl agreed to walk me through the process. She began by leading me into the "heat room," a darkened sarcophagus where they stored the taffy and peanut butter in white plastic bins. You could only see the dim outlines of these bins, and their contents gave off a ghostly shimmer, like something out of *Invasion of the Body Snatchers*. The Abba-Zaba production line itself was humble. "Here's how it works," Karl said. "We cook up a huge batch of taffy, which looks sort of funny when it first comes out of the kettle, like Elmer's glue or something. So then we pull it on this mechanical horse and it gets less sticky and turns opaque. Then feed it into this batch roller, which flattens it out into a thin sheet. Then—"

Karl paused. She bent over to inspect the batch roller. Her brow furrowed. She had noticed a series of names soldered onto one of the rollers.

"Sammy," she called out. "Sammy!"

Sammy was one of the company mechanics, a thin man in a blue cotton jumpsuit who was down at the other end of the line. He came loping over.

"Look at this," Karl said. She gestured at the names. "Did you guys do this?"

Sammy looked at the names (SAMMY among them) and grinned bashfully.

I was worried that something terrible was going to happen now, that Karl was going to fire Sammy on the spot, all because she'd spotted this industrial graffiti, all because I'd come to visit the plant and asked to see the Abba-Zaba line.

But Karl surprised me. She burst out laughing. "Isn't that funny?" she said. "You guys are so crazy."

It struck me that Karl, despite her somewhat type A ferocity, was really a pretty nice woman, and I was relieved to find that she ran a factory where little individualistic flourishes like soldering your name onto a batch roller were to be laughed at, as opposed to what would happen to you at Mars headquarters, for instance, which is that you would be escorted from the plant and shot.

"Alright," Karl said. "So we've got a sheet of taffy coming down the line. This is where the peanut butter comes in." She gestured to the large warming tank beside the batch roller. "The peanut butter gets pumped over from this thing, which is a sort of peanut butter Jacuzzi, and squirted onto the center of the taffy. That part's the most fun to watch. Then the taffy gets folded over, so it's one continuous strip, and it gets fed through the cutter, which forms the seal on both ends."

We headed back to Karl's office, where some time was given over to the standard lamentations of small independent candy companies. Karl was particularly disgusted by the recent adoption of the phrase *real estate* to designate rack space. Because the Big Three had purchased virtually all the retail real estate, Annabelle was often forced to place the Big Hunk in a position where you couldn't even read the name of the bar.

Karl had an aggressive sales staff, and she gave them a good deal of latitude. But there wasn't a lot she could do when it came to the crucial variable, which was price. She feared that Annabelle would be one of the first casualties, should the Big Three begin a price war.

"The big demand from the sales network is always to come out with something new," Karl added. "But that's hard for a company like ours, because we can't really afford to buy a bunch of new machinery. So we do brand extensions. My brother and I did the dark chocolate Rocky Road. And some years ago, we did a Choco-Zaba—"

"I remember those!" I said. "I loved those!"

I was one of the few, Karl noted dryly.

Still, she was always on the lookout for new products. Her most recent brainstorm was an Abba-Zaba with raspberry in the middle. Karl knew that fruit flavors had become really popular and that raspberry topped the list. She settled on the name Raza-Zaba and even began cranking out prototypes. The problem was that, after a few days, the raspberry would start bubbling through the taffy. So her new idea was to combine a green apple taffy with the peanut butter filling.

I had, in fact, *never* heard of people eating green apples and peanut butter. I asked her whether *banana* and peanut butter might be a more familiar combination? (My brother Dave had basically survived adolescence on bananas and peanut butter.)

"Bananas?" Karl said, experimentally.

"You could call it Banana-Zaba," I suggested.

"Banana-Zaba. *Hmmmph*."

I wasn't sure what this meant, this *hmmmph*. Did it mean: Yes, by gum, that might just work! Or did it mean: Who are you again and why did I agree to talk to you? This was never made clear to me, because Karl clapped her hands and went to fetch me some samples and then, politely, sent me on my merry way.

12

A SECOND DEPRESSING BUT NECESSARY DIGRESSION

It was now Thursday, just before noon, and I had covered 4,000 miles in the past four days and seen the inner workings of four different candy factories and survived on a diet that would have made the International House of Pancakes seem like a health food concern. In the course of this journey, I had diagnosed myself with cancer and spent my idle moments in a froth of anxiety. The Republican Party had taken over Congress, so that coddling the rich was the new national pastime, along with watching wars on TV. I had not slept particularly well and, in a few hours, I would have to drive (without a license, ergo, illegally) to San Francisco International Airport to board a red-eye flight back to Boston, then take a taxi to my house, then drive out to Boston College, where a group of students would be waiting for me with their eyes full of cigarette lust and their hearts shut tight as antique lockets, and it would be my job, presumably, to do something about this.

I drifted over the Dumbarton Bridge in a haze of self-pity, gazing at the puny chemical tides rolling in and the tan hills of the East Bay, pleading for rain. Dead ahead was the megapolized mess of 101 and the sad old truth that home is never quite what you left. The trees and streets are all too small and your tired old parents are some newer, haunted incarnation, and you are no longer the child who stared at them in hope of rescue, but an adult responsible for your own sorrow. Just to make sure there was no confusion on this point, my folks had moved across town, to some big new imposter home. The Old Barrel was gone, too. They'd turned it into an old-age home.

It was Freud's belief that people return, inexorably, to the trauma of their childhoods. And he was right. I had spent most of my adult life doing just that, making my best friends into cruel brothers, my bosses into negligent fathers, my sweet, clutching lovers into insufficient mothers. And thereby, fading into my late thirties, I still lived in a condition of aggrieved solitude, as I had so many years ago. I couldn't escape.

I had always imagined that some splendid woman would come along and cure me. Or that my work as a writer, my passionate, empathic accomplishments, would overwrite the bad files of my childhood. And what I realized, as I drove through that light California rain, was that the burden of these great hopes was often too much for me to bear. I feared I would die before I got better. In certain ways, I wanted to die. And, in certain ways, I felt dead already.

I had decided to write about candy because I assumed it would be fun and frivolous and distracting. It would allow me to reconnect to the single, untarnished pleasure of my childhood. But, of course, there are no untarnished pleasures. That is only something the admen of our time would like us to believe. Most of our escape routes are also powerful reminders; and whatever our conscious motives might be, in our secret hearts we wish to be led back into our grief.

There sat the bag of goodies from Annabelle on the seat beside me. I reached in and grabbed myself a Big Hunk so that, even as these dark musings tossed me about, even as I gave myself over to tears, I was also tasting, for the first time in many years, the sweet, cake-batter nougat of that bar and the soft roasted peanuts exploding with flavor on my tongue; chewing and chewing until my jaw ached with the effort.

A LITTLE HIDDEN BOMB IN MY IDAHO SPUD

I don't expect that it will come as any great surprise that the drizzle of that afternoon thickened into a torrential downpour. Nor that winds, sweeping down from the north, created the fiercest storm the Bay Area had seen in several years. Nor that this storm was serious enough to shut down the airport. I did not discover this last fact, however, until I had arrived at my gate.

This left me and 120 other fellow budget travelers playing a restless, grumpy waiting game, the central components of which were whining into cell phones and directing dirty looks at the poor schlubs working the ticket counter. In the course of commiserating with a few fellow passengers, I revealed the purpose of my trip, and before long we were munching our way through the last of the peanut clusters and chocolate-covered pretzels Marty Palmer had given me. A brief jolt of good humor ensued, followed by a plunge into hypoglycemic grumpiness. My connecting flight was at 7 A.M., out of Chicago. I had a 90-minute cushion, but the delay dragged on and on, one hour, two hours. Would they hold the plane in Chicago? Nobody could say. We were supposed to be in the air by 11 P.M., but it was 1:27 A.M. before they began the boarding call.

And here is where the trouble truly began.

I want to make clear that I had grown accustomed, by this time, to the notion that my bags were going to be inspected by airport security. They had been inspected in Boston and Milwaukee and Kansas City and Denver and in Boise, twice. The reasons for this were quite clear. First, all my flights were one-way. Second, having lost my driver's license, I was using an ancient passport, which featured a rather unfortunate photo taken in 1993. In this photo, my face was cloaked in eleven o'clock shadow and my hair was styled in a manner I can only describe as *Upscale Taliban*.

There was a somewhat comical aspect to these inspections, as my carry-on filled with more and more obscure candy bars. The woman in Boise had gone so far as to take these bars out of my suitcase and line them up, one by one, on her inspection table.

"What are these?" she asked me.

"Candy bars," I said.

"Twin Binge," she said. "I've never heard of a Twin Binge."

"Bing," I said. "It's from Iowa."

"What's an Old Faithful?"

"Those are made here in Boise."

She made a noise with her tongue, a soft click intended to express friendly skepticism. And this was just fine. This was Boise, after all. The flight was only half full. There was plenty of time for such shenanigans.

But here in San Francisco, with a long line of passengers blundering down the jet way, and more behind, and the hopes of my connecting flight fading with each passing minute, I was in a less-forgiving mood. The gentleman assigned to inspect my bags was likewise afflicted. He was a short, stout Asian and he opened my suitcase and immediately began raking his fingers through my belongings. I'd brought only a few clothes, and I was wearing most of them, in anticipation of Boston's winter weather. What he was really doing was mauling my sad, strange collection of candy bars.

I wasn't questioning his right to inspect my bag. This was how Americans had chosen to react to the terrorist attacks of September 11. Rather than asking ourselves why a bunch of pious lunatics hated us so much, we hired security guards to sift through our bags. These minor mortifications made us feel safe, and seemed a fair penance for not having been blown up, and for living in such unconscionable comfort.

The other passengers, passing by, looked upon this spectacle with weary curiosity, while I stood on the carpet in my socks. What, I wondered, did he expect to find? Anthrax spores in my Valomilk? A little hidden bomb in my Idaho Spud? Surely, if I'd packed my suitcase with Snickers bars and Hershey's Kisses, there would have been no such mucking about. I felt like saying to this fellow, *Look here: these candy bars you're tossing around, they are a link to our glorious past, to the underdog entrepreneurial spirit that is the finest manifestation of capitalism. It is the bullying voraciousness of the big companies, the need for total worldwide brand domination, that has made America a symbol of greed and an object of derision*. This was probably nonsense, but it felt true at the moment, and it was something to occupy my mind while the rest of the plane filled up with tired travelers.

I managed to catch my connection in Chicago. They held the plane and I scampered through Midway airport and felt an odd sense of good fortune, gratitude even, at the obscene miracles of modern travel.

A FEW FINAL RELEVANT FACTS

1. After visiting the Annabelle factory, I did drive back to Palo Alto, mostly so I could have dinner with my grandfather Gabriel Almond. He was the last of my grandparents, a world-famous political scientist whose wife had, quite abruptly, died on him two years earlier.

My brothers and I spent a lot of time at his house when we were kids, swimming in the pool out back. Of the house itself, I remember most vividly a high cupboard in the kitchen where he and my grandmother kept cookies in a variety of metal boxes whose precise shapes and colors I can still see if I close my eyes. He had something of a sweet tooth, in other words, which he had passed down to his son Richard, and on down to me. I should note that the adoption of a brown spaniel puppy named Snickers had provided him immeasurable solace as a widower.

Dinner was fine. Gabe was a man of considerable charm and he took an interest in my literary pursuits, having been an exceedingly (annoyingly) prolific writer himself. But afterwards, as I drove him back to the little apartment where he had recently moved, a cloud of despair descended on us both. He was depressed by the disappearance of his wife and the home they had made together. The various medications intended to soothe his heart had gummed the powerful gears of his mind. He was too tired to pretend otherwise. Outside, the storm was outrageous. The wind knocked at the windows and made the panes moan. We sat for a while in that darkened apartment and it felt to me as if the keepers of our sadness, those lonely little men who live behind the heart, were calling out to one another: *I am here! I am here! Are you there? Are you there?*

"What's this new project about?" Gabe said finally.

I told him it was about candy bars. But I didn't know if I could explain what I was really getting at: that candy had been my only dependable succor as a child, that it had, in a sense saved my life, that I hoped to draw a link between my personal nostalgia and the cultural yearning for a simpler age, but that, in the end, the laws of the candy world were the laws of the broader world: the strong survived, the weak struggled, people sought pleasure to endure their pain.

Snickers whimpered in his sleep and Gabe reached down to rub his neck.

"Actually," I said, "you make a cameo in the book."

"Is that so?"

I told him the Necco story, how he used to send his oldest son out with six cents to buy the Sunday *New York Times* and how his son would lose a penny down the sewer so he could buy himself Necco wafers.

"Did he?" Gramps gazed at me with his soft brown eyes. "I didn't know that." He slowly yielded himself to a smile, the last one of his I would ever see. "Well, good for him."

2. Back in Boston, I decided to throw a candy-tasting party. I felt it was important that my friends have a chance to taste the strange harvest of my journey. I went so far as to slice the bars into bite-size pieces and lay them out on a cutting board. My fantasy was that people would sample each piece and offer witty bons mots, which I could then steal and use for this very book. Unfortunately, I run with a pretty flaky crowd, sweet people to be sure, but not terribly organized. There was also some drinking that happened and some smoking of pot, and this tended to *impair the evaluative process*. My own notes from the party are not much help to me now. Here is a sample:

blair says u-no like crayon
nice finish (george)
spud spackle, yeah, spackle
I caulk the line (johnny cash?)

Much of the focus of the party was on the unique shape of the Twin Bings. Comparisons were made, both verbal and visual, to the male reproductive organs. I let it slip that Marty Palmer referred to legumes as nutmeats (this seemed germane) and things went downhill from there. I woke the next morning to find that the remains of my candy bars had been arranged, on my kitchen table, in a pornographic tableau.

There was, however, one happy by-product of this gathering. In a moment of freak inspiration, I decided to place a Haviland Thin Mint between two pieces of a dark chocolate Kit Kat. What happened was this: my teeth sent the crisp cookies plunging into the gooey mint, the two chocolates melted into a bittersweet swirl, and my tongue—my tongue went into multiple orgasms. It was the very day after this party that I decided to buy an entire case of Kit Kat Darks—twelve boxes of 36. When I went to pick up this case from a local candy wholesaler, the receptionist told me her phone had been ringing off the hook with requests. Hershey's had discontinued production, of course. Nonetheless, the bar had achieved cult status.

3. Several weeks after my visit, on Christmas Day in fact, my grandfather died. So I got on a plane and flew back to California for the memorial. This was a somber event, full of the sort of muffled sorrow and confusion that ensues when a patriarch dies. That night, I drove with my older brother, Dave,

up to his home in Napa. I wanted to visit my nephews, Daniel, age two and a half, and Lorenzo, fourteen months, or, as they are generally referred to these days, the Wrecking Crew. (Dave prefers the designation Team Head Contusion.)

Strangely, almost creepily, Dave has never shown much interest in candy. Even as a little kid, I can remember him eating half a candy bar and then simply losing interest. I remember this because I was always hoping to chickenhawk his remains and because I was continually thwarted in this endeavor by Dave, who, come to think of it, may have been feigning disinterest simply to torture me. But no, he really is one of those sad cases who feels no sense of urgency in the presence of candy. Worse still, his wife, Lisa, has been pretty hardcore about not allowing the Wrecking Crew to eat processed sugar. My concern, obviously, is that the freak bloodlines are looking pretty watery right about now. My saving grace is that Daniel recently discovered jelly beans. I, of course, had noticed the sign for the Jelly Belly factory (FREE TOURS DAILY!) just a few miles outside of Napa.

The next day, Dave headed off to the clinic where he works as a doctor and Lisa and I spent the morning trying to keep the Wrecking Crew from killing one another, themselves, us. In a moment of unexpected laxity, Lisa agreed to take the kids on an expedition to the Jelly Belly factory. I had imagined we would be allowed down onto the factory floor to watch the machines bang out beans. But the tours were actually conducted by means of video presentations. The Wrecking Crew was not really at the point where it processed information passively. Which is to say: It needed to be in motion. It needed to touch things. It was not prepared to sit quietly and watch a video on the intricacies of the starch mogul. At one point, Daniel, in a heroic (if errant) attempt to reach the factory floor, opened a door marked EMERGENCY EXIT and set off a bloodcurdling alarm, causing both him, and then Lorenzo, to start bawling.

Here again, the gentle reader might fairly claim that freak disaster has risen up and squashed freak joy. But this trip was actually something of a turning point for me. Not that I enjoyed seeing the Wrecking Crew in anquish, those smooth cheeks flushed and shimmering. Such naked hurt! Such soft soft hearts! I wanted to snatch them up and carry them away from the alarm, the sourpuss tour guide, the terrible indignities awaiting them. But that wasn't an option. The basic provisions of life include a certain portion of sadness. Against this, we have only the love we grant one another, and the love we grant ourselves. And so Lisa and I picked the boys up and brushed away their tears and carried them as far as we could, to the end of the factory tour, where they were each awarded a bag of jelly beans. The effects were instantaneous. Daniel wriggled from his mother's arms and performed an impromptu Dance of the Freak. Lorenzo began to lick his bag.

Downstairs, the Crew, restored to a state of relative equilibrium, insisted we stop at the pushcart where a young woman was doling out samples. Daniel watched intently, ferociously, as the Mistress of Bean reached into one of her 40 drawers with a tiny silver scoop and bestowed unto each child a single Jelly Belly. Then he sidled over to the little stool at the end of the cart and climbed onto it and reached matter-of-factly for the nearest drawer, which happened to contain root beer beans. Lisa was busy trying to prevent Lorenzo from eating samples off the floor. The Mistress of Bean was tending to other screaming freaklets. Thus it was left to me to restrain Daniel. I was conflicted. Obviously, this was not a good situation, in terms of discipline, in terms of germs. And yet: you had to admire the kid's form. He had cased out the joint, fair and square, and figured a way in. Root beer was an excellent flavor. In the end, I managed to coax him away from the cart by (somewhat reluctantly) offering him *my* free bag of beans.

Outside, the sky was blue, the traffic was mild, the Crew was in high spirits. I knew there was heavy weather waiting for me back in Boston, where the clouds hung fat with rolling pins of doubt. But, for the first time in months, I felt I could foresee the day those clouds might lift. Something essential was shifting inside me, taking shape, something not unlike faith. America, with its insatiable needs, its flagrant solipsism, was redeeming itself a little, in the form of the Wrecking Crew, who seemed, at that particular moment, as they scampered across the empty parking lot, laughing, their tongues stained a joyful red, to represent the single unassailable blessing of our homeland: the pursuit of happiness as a redemptive impulse.

Daniel, for his part, understood this. He had managed to score two free bags of Jelly Bellies, which he blissfully munched to extinction on the ride home. He spent the remainder of my visit gazing plaintively into my face, repeating a single, solemn incantation: *I want jelly bean.*

There is hope for him yet.

ACKNOWLEDGMENTS

This book would not exist without the concerted enabling of the following freaks:

The entire Almond family, especially Team Head Contusion, for not yet disowning me; Pat Flood, Holden Lewis, Bruce Machart, and Keith Morris for reading the first draft and urging me to write a second; Erin Falkevitz, Tim Huggins, Victor Cruz, Kirk Semple, Tommy Finkel, Dave Blair and Zach Leber for indulging countless vices; Joël Glenn Brenner, Lisbeth Echeandia, Steve Traino, Ray Broekel, and Bob Stengal for answering my idiotic questions; the Big Ruskie, the Gay Lumberjack, and the rest of my various poker freaks for supplying me a small (and undependable) weekly stipend, Eve Bridberg, Chris Castellani, and all the Grub Street freaks for keeping their muse on, my students for putting up with my rant-first-take-questions-later pedagogy; all the Chocolate Gods for so generously (and foolishly) welcoming me into their world, especially Manny De Costa, Chris Middings, Dave Bolton, Joanne Barthel, Carl and David Goldenberg, Marty Palmer, Russ Sifers, Dave Wagers, and Susan Karl. A special shout out to Kathy Pories, Mistress of Pain, for whipping this bad boy into fighting trim, and to anyone who owns or works in an indie bookstore for pimping what you love, and to anyone who still reads—bless you for feeling what you are inside.

FREAK APPENDIX

A woefully-partial-but-nonetheless-well-intentioned list of relevant Web sites.

1. www.candydirect.com
Steve Traino's on-line rare candy depot.

2. www.valomilk.com
A survey of the messiest candy bar in America.

3. www.idahospud.com
Dave Wagers rules my world.

4. www.googoo.com
The official site of the Goo Goo Cluster. Northerners most welcome.

5. www.palmercandy.com
Marty Palmer continues to build his empire.

6. www.lakechamplainchocolate.com
America's finest candy porn, in full color.

7. www.candyusa.org
The National Confectioners Association's main page.

8. snickers99.tripod.com/candymainmain.html
A freak named Mike who is deeply into candy bars, God bless him.

9. www.smm.org/sln/tf/c/crosssection/namethatbar.html
A site that provides a cross section of candy bars and asks you to Name That Bar. (I missed only one.)

10. www.stevenalmond.com
If you have any candy fetishes you wish to post, this is the place.

11. www.sweetnostalgia.com
Lists old-school candy by name, in alphabetical order. Click and buy.

12. www.chocophile.com
A site by and for the hard-core freak. This guy ranks the world's finest chocolate in excruciating, enthralling detail.